What people are saying about

Children's Unexplained ~~~~ ~
Post Materia

For too long, our culture has focus   ~~children~~, and
forgotten that there is an enormous amount we can learn from
them. Donna Thomas' book is essential reading, because it clearly
shows that childhood is a special, spiritual phase of our lives in
which we have easier access to our unexplained experiences. The
book shows that we may need to flip our normal assumptions
about childhood – in some ways, children's experiences of the
world is richer and deeper than adults, and we need to find
ways of regaining their sense of wonder. At the very least, we
need to value children's unexplained experiences, rather than
treating them with disdain. This book is an important step in
that direction.
Steve Taylor PhD, author of *The Leap* and *Extraordinary
Awakenings*

Having researched and taught parapsychology and
transpersonal psychology for many years, I am constantly
privileged with confidential stories of people's "weird"
experiences, which are not weird to me. Very often people are
sharing these exceptional experiences for the first time having
feared all sorts of pathological and diabolical stigma associated
with these taboo subjects. Very often, these experiences
occurred during childhood. So not only do these experiences
often remain subterranean, but they are also woefully under
researched – and so Donna does us and our children a great
service in de-stigmatizing and normalizing these exceptional
experiences in children, and in exploring how these experiences
affect children and the meanings they apply to them.

Dr. David Luke, author, *DMT Dialogues: Encounters with the Spirit Molecule,* **2018**

Unusual experiences of children and adolescents tend to be dismissed as the result of an overactive imagination or, more damaging to them, as pathological.

With Donna Thomas, young people finally have an advocate who does not conduct research on them but with them. In this book, rooted in the most up-to-date scientific expertise and infused by genuine empathy for the youngsters who have those experiences, a new interpretation framework is proposed, based on the most recent findings in the field of consciousness research.

What caring parent will not be delighted to finally have the information needed to better understand their child's unusual perceptions? What responsible professional will not be grateful to have the tools to assess whether therapeutic or pharmacological treatment is really the right way to go?

Children's Unexplained Experiences in a Post Materialist World is a ground-breaking work with the potential to fundamentally transform the current clinical practice. It is also a must-read for anyone seeking insights into those unusual phenomena that their children – and they themselves – may one day experience. **Evelyn Elsaesser**, expert of death-related experiences and project leader of an investigation into spontaneous After-Death Communications (ADCs)

Children remind us of the innocence, joy and – too often – the sorrows and trauma of youth. The rich tapestry of human experience starts in childhood and shapes how adults remember our childhood, and experience self and world in the present. Children really are our future selves. In this ground-breaking book Donna Thomas provides a comprehensive review of the history of ideas and research on unexplained experiences in childhood, including her own work, and guides the reader through a mind-opening exploration of what these experiences reveal about the nature of human consciousness in a post-materialist world.

James Lake MD, author of *An Integrative Paradigm for Mental Health Care: Ideas and Methods Shaping the Future* (Springer, 2019)

In "A Free Man's Worship", Bertrand Russell (1903) describes the world as it is portrayed within the materialistic worldview that much of modern-day science has adopted:

Man is the product of causes which had no prevision of the end they were achieving; that his origin, his growth, his hopes and fears, his loves and his beliefs, are but the outcome of accidental collocations of atoms; that no fire, no heroism, no intensity of thought or feeling, can preserve an individual life beyond the grave; that all the labor of the ages, all the devotion, all the inspiration, all the noonday brightness of human genius, are destined to extinction in the vast death of the solar system; and the whole temple of Man's achievement must inevitably be buried beneath the debris of a universe in ruins – all these things, if not quite beyond dispute, are yet so certain that no philosophy that rejects them can hope to stand. Yet such a bleak view is challenged by the kinds of experiences that are recounted in this scholarly book and only remains tenable if they are dismissed as a consequence of credulity, misunderstanding or even as pathological. But when those experiences become the norm rather than the exception, then it becomes increasingly difficult to set them aside in these ways. Rooted in the lived experience of young people who have not yet been enculturated to differentiate between what is "true" and what is "false", what is "legitimate" and what is "illegitimate", what is "silly" and what is potentially profound, a compelling case is made that these voices need to be heard respectfully. Donna Thomas outlines the nature of the anomalous (unexplained) experiences that occur (often spontaneously and unexpectedly) to many young people and speculates on their meaning and implications. It draws attention to the tremendous value of adopting a participatory approach that sees the experiencer as an intuitive social scientist who is constantly trying to make best sense of their own experience in a rational and coherent way. This contrasts with a traditional approach that sees the researcher as the expert, and the experiencer as someone to be managed, categorized and accounted for, which runs the risk of simply confirming the researcher's own assumptions and biases, and missing a great opportunity to learn something new. As well as showcasing individual accounts, the book is rigorously researched and seeks to contextualize the material within a wider academic understanding. It addresses the taboo around disclosing anomalous experiences that respondents become aware of from a very early age, and can give support and guidance to parents whose offspring may have reported similar experiences and are struggling to come to terms with them – it is clear that simply ignoring or attempting to suppress them out of fear of reinforcing delusional beliefs can be counterproductive, creating more distress or confusion than it resolves. Children often assume that anomalous experiences are the norm, and it may come as a surprise when they find they are not shared by others. When experiences can be shared in a non-judgmental space that allows them to be interpreted and understood, and parallels can be recognized in the experiences of others, then they can provide the foundation for growth and transformation.

Professor Chris Roe, Director, Centre for Psychology & Social Sciences, University of Northampton; resident of the Society for Psychical Research and the International Affiliate for England of the Parapsychology Foundation; Past President of the Parapsychological Association and past-chair of the British Psychological Society's Transpersonal Psychology Section

Children's Unexplained Experiences in a Post Materialist World

What children can teach us about the mystery of being human

Children's Unexplained Experiences in a Post Materialist World

What children can teach us about the mystery of being human

Donna Maria Thomas

Winchester, UK
Washington, USA

JOHN HUNT PUBLISHING

First published by Essentia Books, 2023
Essentia Books is an imprint of John Hunt Publishing Ltd., No. 3 East St., Alresford,
Hampshire SO24 9EE, UK
office@jhpbooks.com
www.johnhuntpublishing.com/essentia-books/

For distributor details and how to order please visit the 'Ordering' section on our website.

Text copyright: Donna Maria Thomas 2022

ISBN: 978 1 80341 084 5
978 1 80341 085 2 (ebook)
Library of Congress Control Number: 2022930122

A CIP catalogue record for this book is available from the British Library.

Design: Matthew Greenfield

UK: Printed and bound by CPI Group (UK) Ltd, Croydon, CR0 4YY
Printed in North America by CPI GPS partners

We operate a distinctive and ethical publishing philosophy in
all areas of our business, from our global network of authors to
production and worldwide distribution.

Contents

Your children are not your children
They are the sons and daughters of life's longing for itself.
The Prophet, Kahlil Gibran

This book is dedicated to *my* children, my teachers,
my gurus, my heart – Alexandra, Olivia and Zakariah –
thank you. To my special *teacups* and to all the
inspirational children who have taught me
how to research and how to be human.

Preface

On a dark and rainy night in September 1988, a young girl, trapped inside the burning wreckage of a car, began to die. As the car began to ricochet, turning over, with the force of a whirling dervish, the young girl became paralyzed, constrained by a consuming terror. As her stunned body slammed against hard plastic and glass windows, she knew she was about to die. Terror was swiftly replaced by a deep peace that cannot be imagined or described. It held, caressed and dissolved the young girl as she grew, expanding to the length and breadth of the universe. No longer a young girl, she held the wisdom of ten thousand scholars and the stillness of a snow-covered meadow, untouched by human footprints. A collage of images imprinted across her field of awareness, scenes and memories that extended across the fifteen years of her existence. The young girl didn't know if the movie lasted minutes, hours, days or a millennium. Time did not exist here. All she knew was the deepest chasm of love that she felt for friends, enemies, her dysfunctional family, boys who had rejected her, the police who had chased her and the teachers who had belittled and berated her. These beings now dissolving across a divine screen of perception, that lovingly held each version of this young girl. Then, in a swift split second, the whole universe once again became the young girl. A girl in pain and fear, her legs twisted with the bent metal of the front seat, and her face broken and bleeding. As the young girl was dragged from the burning wreckage, through the shards of broken window, the car exploded.

The girl grew into a woman who researches with children and their unexplained experiences. Those experiences that cannot be explained through conventional science. Children who experience themselves as the universe, who talk with dead relatives, who can see the future or can travel outside of their bodies. These are varieties of experience known as *anomalous* or *paranormal* that fall on a spectrum. Experiences that cannot really be explained through mainstream science. Researchers such as Etzel Cardeña, Chris Roe and Stanley Krippner have done extensive studies that attempt to show the totality of human experience that is often ignored in social and psychology scholarship. Why is it that mainstream disciplines such as psychology continue to ignore the existence of these types of experiences? And how does this impact on how people are supported by systems designed to heal? The answer may be found in mainstream beliefs about the nature of reality and how they continue to shape our understandings about being human. This book, therefore, is not only about returning to study unexplained experiences in childhood. It is also a call to consider children's experiences within new and exciting ways of viewing reality: a paradigm of scholarship known as "post-materialist". A narrative that positions consciousness as primary.

As a child experiencer, I write this book in the spirit of reflexivity. Making sure that my own experiences (shared earlier) do not impinge on the experiences of the children I research with. It is hoped that my own experiences bring an element of understanding and open-mindedness that is distinctly lacking for unexplained experiences in childhood. When children's unexplained experiences are studied, they are mainly examined in closed clinical contexts. In this way, researchers start from the view that these experiences are disorders or aspects of illness. The research studies presented in this book did not start from clinical contexts. Instead, these studies began from a place of the unknown. The researcher, children and young people courageously stepped into an under-researched and controversial topic, using methods that are still experimental in social research. It takes great courage for children to share their experiences especially when they are accustomed to being silenced, dismissed, or diagnosed by adults in authority. I appeal to the reader to bear this in mind when you enter the space of children's narratives of unexplained phenomena.

Foreword
by Bernardo Kastrup

When it comes to the mental inner lives of children, our culture has an answer so deeply ingrained it is considered an obvious empirical fact: children are naïve, lack knowledge, understanding, and their experiences and views are never to be taken seriously; for children are yet unformed human beings, yet unprogrammed biological computers that, therefore, have nothing to contribute to our understanding of life, the universe and everything.

It is an unquestionable fact that children lack life experience and awareness of our culture's many narratives about who and what we are, what is going on in this strange business called life, and how best to go about it. But that knife cuts both ways: insofar as our cultural narratives have gotten things right, children are indeed at a disadvantage – in relation to adults – for not yet being aware of our hard-earned consensus answers. But insofar as we've gotten things wrong, the childhood condition represents a precious, ephemeral chance to have an impartial look at things, before cultural contamination closes cognitive doors for the rest of life.

The question then is, how sure are we that we've gotten things right? For on the answer to this question rests the potential value of uncontaminated childhood perspectives, inexperienced and uneducated as they may be. I may have an opinion on the matter, but I prefer to relate an incontrovertible fact: every generation in the long and eventful history of Western thought has considered itself right, and all previous generations wrong. We are no exception: again, we think that only our generation has gotten things more or less right, and everybody before us was wrong. Our ancestors were – or so we are led to think – naïve simpletons. Just think of the "silliness" of alchemy or the "fantasy" of Lamarckism.

So, what gives us confidence that, unlike every previous generation that has thought itself right – just as we think ourselves right today – and yet turned out to be wrong, we will be the historical exception? Frankly, nothing. It is more than likely that we, too, will be proven wrong and become the subjects of warm and loving condescension by our descendants. And this is just one reason why it would be smart for us to remain seriously alert to those bright – if unreliable – flashes of impartiality expressed by our children's yet uncontaminated relationships with themselves and the world.

Another reason has to do with a few important things we now know about our own cognitive apparatus. The human intellect – our ability to think symbolically, that is, to replace elements of reality with linguistic concepts and abstractions, thereby working out models, theories, making predictions, and so on – has been around for just fifty thousand years or so (some would say thirty thousand). On an evolutionary scale, this wasn't yesterday; it wasn't even a minute ago: it's just happened. To imagine that this extraordinarily immature intellect is already capable of producing secure answers to the great questions of life is beyond naïve; it is preposterous.

It is true that we can predict, with a fair degree of confidence, many of the observable *behaviors* of nature – such as when eclipses will happen, how computers will react to commands, how drugs will affect a given medical condition, and so on – but that says precious little about our understanding of what nature *is*, including ourselves as parts of nature. You see, a five-year-old kid can become a world champion playing a computer game, because the kid knows how the game *behaves*. Yet the kid doesn't understand what the game *is*, including all the complexity of the electronics and software involved. In a sense, our entire culture is like that kid: we can play the game of technology to wondrous effects – true world champions have we become – but that says very little about our understanding of what nature *is*. Such a realization places us on par with our children in this regard.

But there is another regard in which our children may have a broader perspective than we do: our culture's reliance on the intellect – on conceptual reasoning – has obfuscated other, much older and more mature cognitive faculties. For countless living beings have walked this earth for billions of years without an intellect. During all that time they have engaged with their environment and each other. So they, too, *cognized* nature; just not conceptually. They, too, relied on cognitive faculties evolved and fine-tuned over the eons at great cost to themselves. And today, we reserve a couple of special, catch-all terms for those faculties: intuition and instinct.

But we – our intellects – pooh-pooh intuition and instinct: the former is notoriously unreliable, while the latter is unacceptably coarse; or so the story goes. True as this may be, it is also a terribly biased view, for the inadequacy of intuition and instinct is a self-fulfilled prophecy of almost exclusive reliance on the intellect. A muscle never used is a muscle that atrophies. A cognitive faculty pooh-poohed and disregarded for so long loses its sharpness and sinks into the most obscure regions of the mind, forever lost in darkness. So much so that, today, most of us can no longer distinguish true intuition from wish-fulfilling biases, anxiety-induced expectations, and arbitrary guesswork. And so we attribute to intuition and instinct the failures and unreliability of the latter.

But our children are yet unaffected by these biases. Our culture hasn't yet had the time to dissect away the fulness and richness of their natural cognitive inheritance. Children are still close, in time and experience, to the source of life and reality. They can still *feel through their roots*, which are sunk deep into the warm and moist ground of being. The airy clouds of conceptual reasoning haven't yet forced them to constantly look up to the sky of theory, thereby forgetting the roots through which they are *directly acquainted* with nature. Their biases are still just beginning to form and haven't yet overwhelmed other modes of cognition, other intuitive, instinctual views of the self, of what can or cannot be true, of what is or isn't plausible, and so on. The fountainhead of natural experience still flows uncontaminated in their inner lives. No aspect of that experience is filtered out capriciously or arbitrarily, so to conform to some culture-bound worldview. Children haven't yet forgotten – for they aren't yet overwhelmed with the myriad conceptual narratives we've come to mistake for facts – what feels natural and even self-evident to a truly impartial mind.

To make my views in this regard more alive and concrete, I shall relate something from my own childhood: when I was nine or ten years old, for a period of six months or so, I would regularly have an experience I never forgot: the thought would suddenly assail me that I was... well, *just me* and, therefore, I *wasn't* the other people and the world I saw around me. This thought, while conceptually undeniable, came accompanied with an overwhelming feeling of bafflement, amazement, even unreality, impossibility. It violated something innate in my mind. The resulting cognitive dissonance was palpably painful, for a growing part of me *knew* that, indeed, I *couldn't* possibly be the other people and things around me, could I? But another, older, deeper, non-conceptual part of me – which I couldn't give words to – also knew, *with absolute clarity, that I was my entire world*. I distinctly remember a literally cold shiver slowly running down my spine every time the thought assailed to me. Eventually, I got used to it and the cognitive dissonance faded away. That was the moment when I accepted the *conceptual* answer provided to me by culture, and already built into the language I spoke, over the *felt intuition* that used to run through my entire being.

It was only decades later, through exploring the conceptual, intellectual path of cognition until its ultimate implications, that I realized my natural intuition was right all along: there is no personal "me"; there is only nature, and what I call "me" is merely a segment of that indivisible natural unity. My child-self was right all along in that regard, which immediately raises the question: in what *other* regards might it also have been right? Do I even remember how it viewed life and the world? Today, I deliberately spend much time and energy in trying to rescue my child-self from the obscure, repressed antipodes of my mind, so to be better informed by its language-free, unbiased perspectives, as well as its vitality and unending curiosity.

This is not to say that we should place our children on epistemic altars, thereafter following their whims as if they were the word of an all-knowing divinity; that would be silly. But just as silly is the opposite mistake: to arbitrarily disregard uncontaminated, intuitive, even instinctive perspectives on nature that are billions of years older than the conceptual intellect and its narratives. Ironically, we now find ourselves in a peculiar situation where only in the young, fresh minds of children can we find the oldest, most mature perspectives. For only the young embody the primordial perspective nature has of itself; perhaps a seeming contradiction that, for our sake, we must see through.

It is in this latter sense that I believe this book is desperately needed and urgent: it reinjects into our cultural dialogue a perspective we have arbitrarily – and to our own detriment – casted out. May it be as nurturing to you as my precious childhood memories have been to me.

Bernardo Kastrup
Veldhoven, the Netherlands, July 2022

An Introduction

"I don't believe in things like that – fairies or brownies or magic or anything. It's old-fashioned." "Well, we must be jolly old-fashioned then," said Bessie.

Enid Blyton, *The Folk of the Faraway Tree* (1946)

Enid Blyton wrote about children speaking with fairies and flying off to different lands during the 1930-40s, a time of global war and economic depression. The rise of progressive modernism saw Blyton's books removed from library and school shelves due to elitist, sexist and racist language, unfortunately found in books written at this time. The popularity of Blyton's books is with the spirit of magic, of children's intuitive engagement with nature, meetings with strange beings and realms beyond the ordinary. What may have been lost through post-modern progression is our capacity to be comfortable with tales about the fairy folk, whispering trees and the unknown. In this introductory chapter, I explain why it has become so important to write a book about children and their "unexplained" experiences in a post materialist world. As we move again into a time of global chaos that sees people suffering on a mass scale, whether through war, poverty or inequality, the need to remember our human potential has never been greater. Children and their unexplained experiences can remind us.

Just as our own wisdom has been forgotten, so too have children, in scholarship that seriously studies unexplained experiences, the nature of reality and consciousness. The book addresses this oversight by representing and exploring unexplained experiences in childhood. From the deep past to the present day, across different spaces, cultural narratives and institutional imperatives, children's unexplained experiences will be considered. What separates this book from others that courageously deal with children and unexplained experience is the scope of phenomena explored; and the aim to explain these kinds of experiences within ground-breaking scientific theories and philosophy. This new body of scholarship is referred to as post materialist – a group of philosophers, scientists and scholars who are flipping reality over 360 degrees and proposing that consciousness is the ground of all things. This has huge implications for how we understand who we are as human beings and how we experience self, others and the world. Language can create a heap of troubles for representing accurately our subjective and collective experiences. That's why through this introduction, I examine the term "unexplained" experience and why it has become the preferred choice of word to use to refer to "unusual" experiences. It is also why I pay attention to language and symbol throughout the book. The chapter ends with an overview of the book. This way, the reader can choose which sections they would like to read, not read, start from or end up.

Why Write this Book?

If Bessie reported her experiences of "fairies, brownies and whispering trees" to an adult from the 21st century, she may well be diagnosed with a mental health disorder and prescribed medication. As an adolescent girl, not a younger child, fantasy and imagination would not be an alternative explanation for Bessie's experiences. Many children report experiences of engaging with nonhuman beings, travelling to other worlds, flying (out of body experiences) and conversing with trees. Children will share their own experiences throughout the book, experiences that are very real to them. "Just because someone else doesn't experience it doesn't mean it isn't real," is what I often hear from children. The reality and meanings that children assign to their unexplained experiences are not often taken seriously by well-meaning adults. When they are taken

2

seriously, because children or parents have sought support, children's unexplained experiences can be categorized as mental illness or disorder.

As a vulnerable group, children are at the behest of adults' decision-making about their own experiences, selves, bodies and minds. Children have unrecognized capacities to understand and philosophize how they experience self, others and the world. Although the book is written *about* children for adults, it is relayed through the voices, images and insights of children. With the aim of carving out new ways of thinking and being with children, for adults, carers, scholars and professionals. Together, as adults who were once children, who at times may have found themselves in crisis, silenced or misunderstood, we can start to explore and shape new understandings to support children. As beings in-their-own-right *now* and in their becoming as our future generation. Children can teach us, remind us and support ongoing enquiry into the mystery of being human and the nature of reality.

Defining "Unexplained Experiences"

There is no suitable word to define certain types of human experience that go beyond conventional ideas about what is *normal*. Each word betrays the nature of experience by ordering and categorizing something we still know very little about. Subjective experience that is often viewed as simple or mundane, can be equally mysterious. These are experiences that we often miss, such as feeling the rain touch our faces or the sensation from taking a sip from a cold glass of water. Mainstream science still cannot explain how subjective experience emerges or how we each experience the same things in different ways. Dominant scientific ideologies such as physicalism (and varieties of science that stem from this) suggest that experience arises from physical objects made from matter. This hypothesis or claim has not yet been evidenced, as scientists struggle to solve The Hard

Problem of Consciousness.[1] In other words, to solve the mystery of how subjective experience or consciousness emerges from physical things. I discuss these ideas more in later chapters.

Ironically, many studies about consciousness and subjective experience do not involve everyday people. The very agents from which consciousness allegedly arises. When people are involved in scientific studies, those that examine cognition, perception, and the brain, they are often treated as research objects, rather than co-producers of knowledge about their own living experiences. This is largely a result of how research is valued in science, with studies that start from the experiences of people, often viewed as soft or nonreliable. Measurement systems are developed from traditional child development theories and psychiatric baselines that produce an idea of *normal*. When children (and adults) experiences do not sit nicely in the normal category, they become non-ordinary, exceptional, paranormal or anomalies. These definitions sustain the idea that human experience (and our self) is limited. These terms suggest subjective experience is understood and has already been explained. Experience is a taken-for-granted fact. As mainstream science has not explained the types of experiences I am writing about, I use the word "unexplained" to refer to children's experiences.

It's Dangerous! Researching Children's Unexplained Experiences

It's a little-known fact that the movement of Spiritualism began with two children, aged 11 and 15 years, and their unexplained experiences. In 1848, American sisters Maggie and Kate Fox reported communicating with the ghost of a man murdered in their home. News of their experiences spread, and they became famous, appearing publicly and attracting large crowds. It was then that Spiritualism's popularity grew across the world.[2] It is ironic, therefore, that spiritualist organizations suggest

4

that giving attention to children's unexplained experiences is "dangerous" because children are easily manipulated.[3] Warnings about the dangers of studying unexplained experiences with children can be heard in other contexts too. Some scholars and other professionals claim that unexplained experiences reported by children are illogical, irrational, uncritical and foolish.[4]

There's no doubt that children and adults can be deeply influenced by film culture and social media. If you venture into the realm of TikTok, you will find thousands of videos created by young people that share paranormal paraphernalia, ranging from stories about their own experiences, urban legends and tales of horror. Research shows TikTok users tend to be *tweens*, children aged between 8-12 years who can negotiate boundaries between the public and private very well.[5] Tweens and teens are a lot more online savvy than we give them credit for. However, what I have seen so far has left me a little shaken. There is a clear interest from young people in the paranormal, possibly no different from our own dalliances with the unknown in our tween years. My own research has involved exploring the #teens#paranormal. As I scrolled along, stories began to evolve into sophisticated videos of haunted dolls, skinwalker dogs, demonic faces in pools of water (at this point even I wanted to turn it off but bravely carried on). Then came the experiments. Young people advising others how to contact the spirit of a serial killer!

As a researcher who wants to meet children where they are, without labelling or judging their experiences, I feel the tension between a responsibility to raise awareness of these potentially unhelpful activities, and an allowing for children to express and explore their interests and experiences. At one end of the spectrum, we have adults who study children's unexplained experiences in closed clinical contexts. On the other end, children are exploring (in predominantly negative ways) the unknown in online public contexts. Helpful narratives that are based in science, philosophy or transpersonal psychology, for example, are not available to children. Educational curriculum continues to impose mainstream, limited versions of histories, nature and reality – with no room for critical or philosophical thought for children.

Despite media influences, unexplained experiences of children tend to fall outside their own knowledge of people, places and other influences. This can be seen in the literature that looks at past life memories of children, where children report nuanced, reliable and evidential accounts of lives lived before.[6] Children accessing knowledge beyond their usual selves is also known to happen through Near-Death Experiences. Research on children and NDEs is sparse and is normally conducted with adults reflecting on their childhood NDEs. Children's NDEs and past life memories challenge the idea that children's unexplained experiences are a product of sociocultural and media influences, especially those experiences that have no reference point. For example, children (and adults) can report seeing, sensing and hearing phenomena that does not exist in this world. These might be indescribable colors or sounds.

Criticisms that claim children's unexplained experiences as fantasy and shaped through cultural influences cannot account for all experiences. Children's activity on platforms such as TikTok can inflate theories about the inauthenticity of children's reporting. But this activity is distinctly different from authentic accounts of children's unexplained experiences. For example, children who genuinely have an intense experience, such as engaging with a disembodied entity, remain silent about it. Children tend not to report these kinds of experiences for fear of being ridiculed or disbelieved. This can be very different from the showmanship of tweens and teens on social media. That is why it is very difficult to recruit children into studies on unexplained experiences.

As children are researched "on" instead of "with", opportunities to understand these experiences better are often missed. When scholars, professionals and other adults challenge the capabilities of children in knowing and reporting their own experiences, they position themselves as knowing more. This is simply not the case. As I discuss through examples of research studies through the book, adults can be heavily conditioned by social and cultural ways of thinking that can theorize children's experiences in certain ways. From this position, adults who mean well can silence or misrepresent unexplained experiences of children. What many professionals and parents/carers may not realize is that children have legal rights to be heard.[7] A recent literature review I conducted as part of a recent study, evidenced how children's unexplained experiences are predominantly researched in clinical contexts. The review also demonstrated a large body of literature that studied unexplained experiences with adults outside clinical contexts, but not children. Out of nearly a thousand articles, only thirteen examined children and unexplained experiences in non-clinical contexts. Is it dangerous to research unexplained experiences with children? My view is that children are already having these experiences. It may be more dangerous to ignore, silence or diagnose experiences without researching them *with* children. But we need different models for understanding unexplained experiences in childhood, with children having access to new models of thought about self and the universe. A narrative that does not induce fear but a freedom to co-create their selves and experiences. Current thinking has marginalized unexplained experiences in childhood into two distinct models – mental health and psychic kids – both promoting fear and creating unnecessary suffering.

What's in the Book?

Before outlining what's in the book, it's important to note how I use the word "children", in terms of who I'm referring to. I am using children as a blanket term that covers an age span of 0-18 years. Clearly, within this age spectrum there are significant differences. For example, a child of two years and a young person of seventeen years will experience self, others and the world in very different ways. Usually, a clear distinction is made between children and young people. For the purposes of the book, I use the term children to refer to our next generation. I vary use of the terms babies and infants (0-2 years), children (3-12 years) and young people (13-18 years) when writing about different children.

The book is organized to move, from children's unexplained experiences to self and states of consciousness, to arrive at science and philosophy. The first five chapters of the book focus on children's unexplained experiences. In modern society, there are two dominant systems of thought around children's unexplained experiences – mental disorder and psychic kids – each positioning children and their experiences at opposite ends of a spectrum. I begin the book by examining these two grand narratives, asking whether they truly account for unexplained experiences in children. Culture and its relationship to children's unexplained experiences is covered in the early chapters, along with the role of technology in children's lives. Studies into unexplained experiences in childhood, past, present and going forward, make up the first part of the book – asking us to reflect on what we can learn from the past as we return to the unexplained experiences of children.

By chapter 6, the book bridges children's unexplained experiences with the nature of self and states of consciousness. Traditional ways for thinking about *who we are*, are challenged through children's experiences. How children naturally shift into altered states of consciousness, for example through play, is also explored. Children's unexplained experiences are theorized within ideas of a collective consciousness, a transpersonal nonmaterial field, that children have a close and natural relationship with. In the final chapters, the book moves into the fields of science and philosophy, considering the mind-body problem through children's unexplained experiences and medical conditions. The final chapters explore new areas in science and philosophy that could account for children's unexplained experiences in a post materialist world.

Chapter 1

The Grand Narratives of Children's Unexplained Experiences

A recent article published on Kidspot, "Your child could be psychic and here's what to look out for", gives a list of five pointers that measure if your child is psychic. The list includes being highly sensitive to emotional energies, reports of imaginary friends, vivid dreams and nightmares, a fear of being alone in the dark and easily overwhelmed by their environment.[8] Do these experiences really seem so unusual? Each of these experiences can be attributed to normal aspects of childhood and some stages of adulthood too! Viewing these kinds of experiences as *psychic*, only known by the *gifted*, betrays the fact that these experiences are very common. Especially in childhood. Children have experiences that could be considered far more unusual than those presented by Kidspot. In my own research studies, children report speaking with dead relatives, knowing the future and having vivid out of body experiences (OBEs). Even experiences of this type are common for children.

This chapter examines two contemporary ways that are used to think about, and represent, unexplained experiences in childhood. One is the popular cultural narrative of psychic children, the other is the grand narrative of mental health. Why are these narratives *grand*? Language influences how we self-identify and relate to others. In fact, language is a social practice that plays an important role in shaping how we experience self, others and the world. Powerful institutions such as the media and health use different linguistic tools (features of language) to construct and weave big stories about aspects of reality. These tools of language can be persuasive, emotive or factual, such as *nominalizations*, where verbs are turned into nouns to

10

claim truths.[9] Language plays a role in shaping human behavior and constructing our personal inner stories. It's important therefore to first cast a critical eye over the grand narratives that frame how children's unexplained experiences are understood by society-at-large. Returning to unexplained experiences in childhood is a response to children's own narratives, insights and intuitions in a troubling world.

Children, Unexplained Experiences and Mental Health

Studies show that one in five children worldwide experience mental health problems. In 2019, over 350,000 children in England alone accessed mental health services, with only one in five children receiving any support.[10] This disturbing figure reflects globally how children are suffering – and it is a number that is continuing to rise, following the global pandemic. A review of studies that included nearly 90,000 children worldwide, found that symptoms of mental illness (anxiety and depression) had doubled compared with pre-pandemic estimates. Data from the USA suggests that psychosocial problems are rising for children, with increases in both inner and outer problems.[11] Children are negatively impacted by global as well as local crises that affect their inner and outer worlds. Depression and suicide attempts have sadly increased significantly in children across the world. There are a host of social problems thought to intersect with the increasing decline of children's mental and emotional well-being. For example, Australia's fluctuating economy is giving rise to poverty while environmental disasters, such as the recent fires, are creating homelessness for many families. Increased rates of single parenting across Europe have been cited as creating mental distress for children and parents, through loneliness and isolation. Many of these social problems can correspond with how society operates, in ways that divide and separate children from adults, and from their own ways of being in the world (these ideas are discussed more in the next chapter).

Mainstream approaches to treating mental health issues in children tend to be clinical diagnoses and medication. Many academics and practitioners are starting to believe that the medically dominated approach to supporting children does not work. The biomedical model assumes people to be discrete machines, separate from the natural world and from each other. In this way, mental *disorder* is treated as a malfunction within the individual, rather than a reaction to a dysfunctional world. Some commentators have noted the negative impact of western culture on the developing child. Modern culture is premised on scientific narratives that claim the world is filled with dead or inert matter, which is problematic for people, animals and the environment. The increasing number of children in crisis is often blamed on a lack of resources and social issues such as poverty and ill health. There are certainly intersections between social troubles and suffering – but circumstances are not the root cause for children's unnecessary misery.

It's easy for adults to dismiss children's stories about strange happenings, such as imaginary friends, as fantasy. As children grow, moving through the teenage years and into adulthood, imaginary friends are not only taken seriously, but viewed by society-at-large, as symptoms of a disorder. The same experience takes on different meanings. Shockingly, children as young as five are routinely diagnosed, when concerned parents seek support for unusual experiences and behaviors, such as hallucinations, night terrors and obsessive thought disorders. Etiological research investigates the relationship between risk factors and disease or other negative outcomes. Risk factors for children acquiring psychosis or schizophrenia, for example, include cognitive impairment, troubled home lives (including mothers' emotional status), and educational problems at age five.[12] While risk factors and neurodevelopmental issues are correlated, there are still no clear medical definitions of conditions such as psychosis or schizophrenia.

Clinicians claim, by studying children, the origins of schizophrenia in adults can be predicted – identified through indicators such as behavior, emotions, social skills, cognitive and motor development. The first three indicators are closely tied to social life and how children respond to the environment. The latter are biological in nature, linked to errors in the brain. All are fixed within traditional child development models that are also problematic (a point I discuss in more detail in later chapters). Instead of exploring experiences *with* children such as visions (hallucinations) or voice-hearing, they are already predisposed as symptoms or markers of illness across the life course, despite very little understanding of the phenomena. What is interesting is how children who are not diagnosed with any condition are increasingly reporting unexplained experiences:

> What does it mean when a child reports experiencing hallucinations or delusions? Increasing interest in this question has been stimulated by reports that hallucinations and delusions occur among children in the community who do not have childhood schizophrenia, that preadolescent children are able to self-report these symptoms…However, the clinical and theoretical significance of their symptoms is not yet clear.
> Polanczyk et al (2010)

Researchers, by default, try to establish clinical and theoretical explanations for experiences that are referred to as delusional or hallucinations. A better place to start from, would be to unpick what is meant by "delusion" and to ask why these experiences are so common in childhood. Unexplained experiences are already positioned as "symptoms" before the phenomena is explored with those who have an authority about the nature of the experience – children. Recent psychosocial studies suggest that psychotic or unexplained experiences, such as delusions or hallucinations, are experienced by general members of the population. These are known as *psychotic-like experiences* (PLEs) and are viewed as symptoms that are not strong enough to meet the threshold for full diagnosis.[13] A cross-national survey involving 261 people across 18 countries found that many otherwise healthy individuals were reporting histories of hallucinations and delusions.[14] PLEs are shown to be more common in children aged 9-12 years, a time when children experience puberty and transition from one stage of life into the next. There is always a need to identify clinical explanations for experiences such as visions or voice-hearing even when they cannot be described through conventional science. Many adult survivors (of the mental health system) report experiences such as voice-hearing or visions in childhood, that they frame within models of spiritualism, such as mediumship, which they continue to practice into adulthood.[15] Parents' reactions and professional support can be influenced by western clinical and scientific thinking. Mainstream biomedical models have an aversion to suffering and negative human emotions. Recent attention to the impact of suppressed trauma, through professionals such as Gabor Mate,[16] highlights society's compulsion to hide from natural human processes such as grief and death.

In the US and UK, there has been a dramatic increase in medication prescribed to children with concerns growing about giving medication to children for mental health conditions. Worries about informed consent, parens patriae and medicating human experience are now emerging.[17] Reports of negative side effects of medication are also increasing. A recent British news article from 2020, reports how a young male with autism was given antipsychotic medication against his own and his parents' wishes. Both his parents attempted to tell the medical team that their son was allergic to antipsychotic medication.

Their objections were ignored by professionals and their son was administered the medication. No less than 24 hours later, their son was dead.[18] There are similar stories in the news that report cases of incarceration, abuse and death of young people in institutions that are designed to support those with *mental illness*.

I have spoken with nurses who work in high-risk secure mental health units with young people. I wanted to understand their views about the kinds of experiences children have and what might be some of the similarities and differences between unexplained experiences and mental illness. In their view and my own, the experiences seem to have the same qualities (visions, voice-hearing, dissociation etc.), but how they are framed and responded to by adults can make a difference. In the case of young people in secure units, it may be too late to explore their experiences in a meaningful way. "How does it get so bad?" I asked one nurse. His reply solidified my own view, as he spoke about the need to explore experiences with children before they grow into complete distress and confusion. This is different from the popular concept of early intervention that proclaims to cure illness before it spreads. Before we frame or recoil from children's distressing inner experiences, researching with children as part of everyday life could reduce negative and persistent unexplained experiences.

Unexplained Experience or Mental Disorder?

How children and their experiences are treated are framed by policy discourse (language and official documents) that affect the lives of disempowered groups, such as children. A good way to demonstrate this is to include here a small story told by a young person in a study I conducted in 2019:

> So, I was like oh my god so then my dad was like I think you're schizophrenic so then I was like oh my god then maybe these things that I'm seeing are not real so then I was like I won't

say anything because they won't take it seriously.

Emma, aged 16 years

In her story, Emma reports how she feels when she tries to tell her parents about the unexplained events she experiences (seeing beings, premonitions and out of body experiences). Emma brings her father into her story by indirectly representing his words ("my dad was like I think you're schizophrenic"). Her father's reaction is shaped by the grand narrative of mental health that has implications for how Emma understands, shares or silences her experiences. In other parts of her story, Emma describes an inner struggle created by her parents' responses to her experiences. The struggle is between her own experiences and what society is telling her it is (illness/disorder). This type of response from adults in authority can be seen across my own studies, as was children's reluctance to continue to share their experiences. As parents or professionals who work with children and young people, we are exposed to mainstream language, practices and stories that have a very defined view of what constitutes mental illness. When our children, or children we support, start to report experiences that challenge everyday ideas about *normal* experiences and behaviors, we can worry about our child's mental health. For professionals, our work with children is always governed by strict organizational rules and guidelines that can presuppose what is normal and what is not. It is difficult terrain to traverse, and it's helpful to consider what differences there may be between spontaneous experiences and experiences that are catalyzed by suffering.

The fine line between unexplained experiences and mental health disorders has been discussed by researchers such as Phil Borges, an anthropologist and filmmaker who studied psychotic-like experiences of children and how they were understood in First Nation contexts. In a recent TED talk, "Psychosis or Spiritual Awakening?",[19] Borges documented how teenagers were supported through key transitional life stages (such as puberty), mentored by elders and supported by the whole community. Experiences that would be viewed as psychosis in the western world were considered as initiatory and transformational, part of the cycles of death and rebirth (for example, the death of the child and the birth of the teenager). Usually, children who have these kinds of experiences in indigenous contexts go on to become key social figures within their communities. This is a far cry from the destinies of children in the western world, who can become ostracized or incarcerated for the same kinds of experiences. Considering how little we know about the mind, subjective experience and reality, it is astounding how such fixed meanings are ascribed to human experience. The western model of psychiatry and artefacts such as the Diagnostic and Statistical Manual of Mental Disorders (DSM) have fixed human experience within medical categories of disorder. Not only in the western world but across many First Nation and developing countries. Many scholars, psychiatrists, psychologists and service user groups are challenging mainstream psychiatric practice. Calling for social and cultural influences to be considered when supporting mental distress.

Experiences such as hearing voices and hallucinations are included in the DSM as signs of psychosis, personality disorder or schizophrenia. These types of conditions are still not understood very well, in terms of what they are and why they occur. Experiences such as hearing voices and visions are viewed as anomalous or exceptional experiences in disciplines such as parapsychology. A vast amount of data in parapsychology evidence how adults have unexplained experiences that challenge mainstream views of reality. Yet as parapsychology is not yet considered a mainstream discipline, results are not often used to inform policy and practice. There are factors that professionals use to distinguish between unexplained experiences and mental disorders. If the experience causes a child to behave in antisocial ways or creates distress, then unexplained experiences are viewed as illness. Differences are not found in the experiences themselves, rather they are identified by how individuals respond to experiences and how others react. Crisis and distress can open children more to experiences that go beyond the everyday. However, as a culture, we endorse the suppression of unhappiness in children, and often, their feelings (and experiences) are quickly diagnosed as mental illness. James Hillman, a Jungian psychologist notes how "the language of psychology insults the soul... we are all made ill because it is ill."[20] Mainstream psychology can subject children's inner lives to surveillance and measurement through fixed systems of thought. This may explain the rising number of children across the world who are accessing or waiting to access mental health support. Adults who resist medical definitions of children's unexplained experiences have little support or a choice of explanations. Popular culture can provide a different narrative in which children's unexplained experiences can be situated.

Psychic Kids: Children's Unexplained Experiences in Popular Culture

The 1990s saw a surge of all things children and unexplained. In academia, a small number of researchers were writing about unexplained experiences in childhood, such as Ed Hoffman and Drewes & Drucker. Ed Hoffman wrote a book about mystical experiences in childhood that argued for the naturalness of these kinds of experiences.[21] Drewes & Drucker, in 1991, published a bibliography of psi experiences that captured many examples of studies about cognitive abilities in children such as telepathy and precognition. In popular culture, a similar movement emerged that focused on psychic kids or indigo children. Lee Carroll and Jan Tober's *Indigo Children: The New Kids Have Arrived* was a bestseller, catalyzing a barrage of movies, documentaries and networks about indigo children. According to Carroll & Tober, indigo children demonstrate unusual psychological traits such as telepathy, increased sensitivities (such as empathic abilities) and deep creativity. Parents are asked by Carroll & Tober to recognize and celebrate their indigo children, these special children who come in knowing who they are.

Like all cultural myths, there could be elements of truth in Carroll & Tober's indigo children's theories. These types of narratives can be found in the ancient stories of First Nation people such as the Hopi community and their myth of the Rainbow Children, a group of warriors who would contribute to saving the planet. If human beings evolve over time, this might suggest that our cognitive capabilities may increase with each generation. This would mean all children would naturally have these capabilities and not just a percentage of indigo children. Categorizing certain children as special or gifted leads us back to the same issue highlighted earlier through the example of Kidspot. Portraying some children as special if they have psychic or indigo attributes can disregard the naturalness of children's experiences. The Psychic Kids narrative can subordinate some children through labelling some as special and others as ordinary. A carer who proclaims their child is an indigo or psychic and special, may be no different than a parent who states their child is a schizophrenic. As Joseph Campbell reminds us, the waters are muddied between the mystic and schizophrenic![22] Both are fixed ways of thinking, and both are assigning adult meanings onto children's experiences.

Psychic Kids: Children of the Paranormal was a US television series that ran from 2008-2010. The show brought together psychic children with an aim to mentor their abilities. The show's format sees a child psychologist and a psychic, supporting children who have unexplained experiences. *Psychic Kids* is an interesting documentary as it demonstrates how children can have intense experiences, such as mediumship capabilities and healing abilities, that can impact on their lives. The show examines how parents respond to their children's experiences, with frightened mothers, skeptical stepfathers and supportive grandparents, sharing their insights and validating (or not) their children's experiences. Most parents reported fears of their child being mentally ill or being helpless to support their distress and fear.

These are common concerns from parents of children who have intense experiences like those reported in the show. Many parents will take their children to see a medical professional, usually a general practitioner who will then prescribe medication or refer children to a specialist. In some cases, children (young people) will seek medical advice for physical discomfort that they see as part of their unexplained experiences. For example, in the *Psychic Kids* documentary, one girl sought medical help for her frequent migraines. No medical explanation could be found. In my own studies, young people report feeling faint, excessive tiredness, and aches and pains in their bodies. They seek medical advice and undergo tests, only to find that they have no physical issues. Their pains are unexplained. It's unfortunate that these children and their experiences are represented through eerie horror music, dark shadowy film effects and collages of negative quotes. The documentary sensationalizes these children's experiences in ways that can sustain the paranormal fear culture.

Similarly, the language used by the medium who is tasked to support and train children is very unhelpful, adding to the sensationalizing of experiences that cannot be explained. The psychic tells children as young as eight "you're haunted" or you're not allowed to fear. However well-intentioned this may be, this is an example of framing children's experiences in a negative way, that could catalyze further fear and distress. Children's experiences are explained within the paranormal narrative, where they are either captured by negative spirits or *vampired* by other people's energy. If we turn to the movie industry it is clear how unexplained experiences and the unknown are constructed in terrifying ways. With the rise of easily accessible entertainment platforms such as Netflix, never has it been easier for children to access horror movies. Even 12-rated series contain images and references to spooks, spiritual possessions and more. Cult shows such as *The Vampire Diaries* appeal to the romantic, to fashion and significant teen issues to draw in their young audiences. It seems, *Psychic Kids* also appeals to this format.

The most captivating aspects of the documentary can be seen in simple moments, through the basic statements these children make. In episode one, Ahila aged 11 who sees spirits states, "These things are real." This mirrors findings from my own research with children. What is common is how children will try and emphasize that their experiences, to them, are very real. As Melvin Morse noted in a case study published on a six-year-old boy who had an NDE, these experiences are "realer than real."[23] Let us turn to some examples of unexplained experiences identified through recent research studies. Without the eerie music and rolling mist, I now share some *small counter-narratives* from several of my own studies with children.

Examples of Unexplained Experiences of Children

The examples in this section come from different research studies that explore with children unexplained experiences, the nature of self and connections with others.

Out of Body Experiences

Many people report out of body experiences. An OBE is an experience in which a person views the world from a place outside of their own body. A feeling of having left the body often accompanies this shift in perspective. Features of an OBE include sensations of floating, travelling to distant locations and observing the physical body from a distance.[24] From a neuroscience perspective, OBEs are neural processes in the brain that have gone awry. Explanations such as a lack of oxygen to the brain or the release of certain neurochemicals have been used to challenge the idea of the OBE experience. From the perspectives of people who have them, OBEs are a very real experience that provoke changes in how people see themselves and reality. The following examples are taken from different research studies. Aisha is aged fifteen and lives with a life-limiting condition. Aisha uses a wheelchair as she has lost functioning in her legs and some of her upper body. Michael is 10 years old and has a history of reporting past life memories and significant empathic abilities.

Weightless

Aisha was not a stranger to being in hospital because of her condition. This time, Aisha had been admitted to hospital to have an operation. The procedure went well for Aisha and she found herself in a private room. Aisha describes how she drifted in and out of sleep after the operation. By the second day, Aisha reports feeling especially tired. Being bedbound as Aisha could not physically move without her wheelchair, she relaxed into the bed. As Aisha closed her eyes, she experienced getting up from the bed. Now, this is a simple and usual experience – but not for Aisha, who needs assistance to do the things those of us with use of our bodies can take for granted. As Aisha rose from the bed, she felt weightless. It felt strange to move around and Aisha felt as though she didn't have a body – yet had the "strange" sensation of feeling what it may be like to use "her feet". Aisha described a feeling of lightness and reported seeing machinery (a heart monitor) in her room that was positioned outside her usual periphery vision. As Aisha experienced moving around her hospital room, she began to feel something pull her back to her body. "I guess the word would be spirit," is how Aisha described the force that pulled her back towards the bed.

Up on the Roof

Michael was 10 years old when he had his first experience of camping. As Michael snuggled into his sleeping bag, he fell into a deep sleep. Or so his mother thought. In the morning Michael told his mother about how he had woken during the night. He explained how he wasn't in his sleeping bag, instead he found himself on the roof of the tent, looking down at his and his mother's bodies. Michael described feeling weightless and peaceful as he floated up to the roof of the tent.

Hearing Voices

Robots

At the age of five, Kimberley began hearing "helpful" voices. The voices would arrive when Kimberley was feeling unsafe or insecure. They would reassure Kimberley, telling her that everything would be OK. Kimberley appreciated the helpful voices and thought it was something that happened for everyone. By the age of seven, Kimberley experienced periods of absence and couldn't remember parts of her day. Teaching staff at her school would notice and Kimberley was eventually diagnosed with epilepsy. The voices disappeared when Kimberley began taking medication for epilepsy. "I really missed the voices," reflected Kimberley as they had supported her through many difficult moments. Kimberley described the voices as "little robots". When we explored this more, we discovered that the voices were not robotic. They were slowed down in normal space-time. Kimberley suggested that the time difference meant that they came from a distant place to support her. What is interesting is that as Kimberley grew older, she began to have conversations with her deceased grandmother. These could be signs of mediumship capabilities. Often, adult mediums report these types of experiences in childhood.

Image 1: Helpful Voices

Precognition

Precognition is the ability to obtain information about a future event, unknowable through inference alone.[25] The ability to know the future conflicts with our usual understanding of time flowing from past to future. Precognition in children seemed to behave as a warning to protect them or others from danger, harm or stress. In some cases, premonitions came to foretell someone's death. Here are two stories:

The Missing Letter

Lebron was five years old when I first researched with him. A bright and loving young boy, Lebron had been recently diagnosed with a rare form of Narcolepsy with Cataplexy. Lebron's mother, Kristina, reported how her little boy had a history of seeing beings in the house (animals and other nonhuman beings). One morning, a family friend contacted Kristina. In the conversation, the friend mentioned that she had lost an important letter that was needed. Kristina, though concerned for her friend, didn't give the missing letter much thought when she ended the call. That night, Lebron began to talk about the friend that had called his mother. He told Kristina where her friend would find the missing letter.

Stunned, Kristina pondered on what Lebron had said. How did he know about the letter? It must be that he overheard the conversation, she thought. The following morning, the friend contacted Kristina. Curious, Kristina enquired into the missing letter, asking her friend if it had been found. Sure enough, the letter had been found. In the same place that Lebron had predicted.

The Car Crash

Grace was a pragmatic girl aged 17 and studying for a career in medicine. Grace reported a wealth of unexplained experiences over the time I spent with her. One evening, Grace sat waiting for her friend to call to arrange a trip out. Grace had been looking forward to spending time with friends, after a long day at college. But as Grace sat waiting for the call, she began to feel nervous. The nervous feeling turned into dread. The phone rang and Grace answered with the dread growing stronger. As Grace connected the call, she had a vision of a mangled car wreck and heard a voice telling her not to go out with her friends. It was so powerful, Grace gave her apologies to her friend and stayed at home. A few hours later, she received a call. Her friends had been involved in a car accident. Luckily, all Grace's friends were safe. This may not have been the case if Grace had been in the car too. With too many passengers, the accident could have been much worse.

Shared Dreams and Lucid Dreams

Fariba Bogzaran, author of *Integral Dreaming*, writes about the different kinds of dreams people can have. These categories extend beyond the commonly known "lucid dream" and include dreams of precognition and telepathy. Bogzaran also examines "shared dreams" where two different people can experience themselves in the same dream. This is what happened with two teenagers I interviewed and a young boy and his grandmother:

The Forest

Chris woke up in the morning, feeling fresh, glowing from a beautiful dream he had during the night. In his dream, described as "vivid" and "very real", Chris found himself in a beautiful forest. "All the trees and grass had really rich colors," reported Chris. He then described looking up and seeing his girlfriend standing there. Chris described his girlfriend as "the most beautiful thing I had ever seen." Feeling an overwhelming rush of love, Chris reached out and held her face in his hands. After Chris awoke from this dream, his girlfriend Lottie, who was sleeping in the same bed, woke up too. "Chris," she beamed, "I've just had the most beautiful dream." Lottie began to describe how she was standing in a beautiful forest, with luscious colors. She then saw Chris who took her face into his hands.

Grandma and the Monster

Jack, aged three, had been suffering with vivid nightmares involving monsters. His mother had started to worry as Jack's sleep pattern was becoming disrupted. Jack shared a close bond with his grandmother, and she was sad to hear that he was suffering from nightmares. "I'll come and sort that monster out," said Grandma to Jack, hoping to reassure the tired little boy. That night, Jack found himself in the same nightmare, being chased by a large, black shadow monster that appeared out of dark tunnels in the ground. This time, instead of running, Jack turned around. As the monster emerged from the tunnel, Grandma appeared and took care of the monster, making it disappear into a cloud of smoke. Now, we could conclude from this story that Jack's subconscious mind conjured Grandma to deal with the monster. But the story does not end there. That same night, Grandma had a dream. In her dream she found herself lucid, she knew that she was in a dream. Grandma also had a sense that this was not her dream, as she looked around the landscape. She could hear screams and recognized them as belonging to her grandson, Jack. Moving towards the screams, Grandma found herself at the edge of a dark tunnel, where a large black monster was emerging. She could see little Jack running, then stopping to turn round. Their eyes met, indicating that Jack was lucid too. With the fury of a mother protecting her offspring, Grandma melted the monster with the force of her own energy. She woke, sweating and brushing the dream off as her worries over her grandson. That day, Jack told Grandma that he saw her dissolve the monster in his dream. It's safe to say that Grandma was left speechless!

Engaging with Beings

Reports of ghosts and apparitions are very common. The best stories involve specters and spirits who take various roles as villains, guardians or wise advisors. Having visions or engaging with beings others cannot see are experiences regarded as hallucinations in medical contexts. For younger children, unseen beings have been classified as "imaginary friends", the term bringing a certain nostalgia and comfort. Children that I have researched with, including teenagers, report engaging with unseen beings. They can be frightening or supportive, float by or engage with children. Some take the form of humans while others are not recognized as human or animal. Here are three stories from Daisy aged four, Yasmin aged nine and Jane aged 17 years, about their own encounters with beings others cannot see.

Lady on the Ceiling

Daisy was four when she reported a strange lady flying around her bedroom. Daisy had been staying with her grandparents. All week, Daisy had been struggling to settle, claiming she was frightened from the monsters in her bedroom. Tired from another restless night, Daisy and her grandparents were eating breakfast. "I saw a lady in my room last night," reported Daisy.

Her grandparents assigned this latest report to the monsters in the bedroom. But Daisy pressed on. "This lady was on the ceiling then on the top of my door looking at me." It was the first time that Daisy had offered any other details about her night-time encounters. The following week, Daisy returned to stay with her grandparents. Daisy's grandmother had decided to sort out the photo albums. As Daisy scurried over to check on her grandmother's activities, she stopped and squealed. "That's the lady," exclaimed Daisy. "Which lady?" asked her grandmother. "The lady in my bedroom," stated Daisy. The lady that Daisy had identified was her great-grandmother.

A Helping Hand

Yasmin was a confident, bright and happy girl. I was contacted by her mother as Yasmin reported seeing beings. Some of these beings made her feel frightened, such as the "black man" who she had seen in her house and outside too. I conducted some research activities with Yasmin to explore her experiences and understand how she made sense of them. Yasmin reported that not all her experiences were unpleasant. Each night, Yasmin reported how she is visited by a being that she cannot see. The being holds her hand and this helps her to fall asleep. Yasmin does not feel frightened, in fact she finds this presence reassuring. When I asked Yasmin about her own ideas about these experiences, she explained that it is very normal. Perhaps these kinds of beings are always around, it's just that we all can't see them.

A Man in my House

Jane spoke in a matter-of-fact way about the beings that she encounters in her home. Some interact, moving chairs and other pieces of furniture. While others appear to glide through different rooms in the home. One day, Jane was watching TV in the lounge. She describes two large patio windows that lead to an extra room. "I glanced up," said Jane, "and a man, about 40 was just stood there, staring right at me!" Jane looked back at the figure that she describes as humanlike and very real. She then watched the figure slowly dissolve and eventually disappear.

A Return to Children's Unexplained Experiences?

How could we know if Jane's experience was *real*? Can we trust Jane's small account above as evidence that she interacted with a disembodied being? This question could apply to most examples presented throughout the book. Some are clarified by other witnesses, such as the case of the missing letter or great-grandmother and the photo album. While other case studies rely solely on the reports of children. The question of whether an experience is *real* appeals to traditional research thinking that calls for measurement and empirical validity. Such questions about the reality of these types of experiences require more detailed discussion about what is meant by reality (I examine this more in later chapters). The experiences reported by children are very real for them, to the point where they can affect their relationships with others and the world. There are subtle indications that point to the authenticity of children's reporting. Signs such as emotions that arise, conviction in their reporting strategies and their uncanny insights about the nature of reality. Children share their experiences at the risk of being shut down or called crazy. There are no rewards for children who relay fantasies about hearing voices or floating out their bodies. Many younger children are not aware that these kinds of experiences are unexplained or unusual, they are normal and experienced by everyone from their perspective. A return to children's unexplained experiences is crucially important as we navigate a world in crisis that sees children diagnosed or sensationalized for their unexplained experiences.

Despite the realness for children, adults position children's unexplained experiences into different frameworks of understanding. This chapter has focused on two modern and dominant narratives, mental health and psychic children. Narratives are intertextual, meaning they contain narratives from other social domains. For example, the psychic children narrative is interwoven with discourses of the media, film and new age thinking. While the mental health narrative is pervaded by education and economics. Recent moves to normalize children's experiences such as voice-hearing are valuable but are still located in the narrative of mental health – where well-being is measured against how well children can function in a very dysfunctional social system. We need a different narrative in which to locate children's unexplained experiences, one that accommodates children's meanings and resistance to institutional explanations. A narrative that does not separate the enquiry from wider questions about who or what we are as human beings. Culture determines how grand narratives unfold. In the next chapter, I examine the relationship between culture and children's unexplained experiences.

Chapter 2

Culture, Children and Unexplained Experiences

These crowds and crowds of little children are strangely absent from the written record... there is something mysterious about the silence of all these multitudes of babes in arms, toddlers and adolescents in the statements men made about their own existence.
Laslett (1974)

In May 2021, the shocking discovery of the remains of 215 First Nation children, students at a residential school, were found in unmarked graves.[26] The residential schools in Canada represent a callous legacy of the state attempting to *assimilate* First Nation children into western cultural values. The rationale for the residential schools was based on *civilizing* the First Nation communities. With residential schools closing as recently as 1996 approximately 150,000 Indian, Inuit and Metis children attended these residential schools.[27] First Nation communities such as the Inuit people believe all living and nonliving things have a spirit. Even forces of nature like the wind or the seasons are spirit. Children (and their communities) were forced to concede their spiritual beliefs and practices to accommodate western doctrines – western beliefs that are so very far removed from their own origins, as this chapter will start to show. My own studies are starting to evidence how children's unexplained experiences, and how they are understood, are heavily intertwined with the cultural values in which they are located. This is problematic when the dominant cultural narrative states that some of their experiences are not possible.

Culture plays an important role in how children's unexplained experiences are understood and supported. As discussed in the first chapter, children's unexplained experiences are often framed within a mainstream narrative of mental health, that is deeply informed by the materialist paradigm. In this chapter, I examine western culture more deeply, considering the influences that continue to inform how children's unexplained experiences are understood in the modern world. When one starts to examine old western cultural narratives, a comparison can be made between "the old European religion" and the cultural myths found in non-western societies. I examine this connection through this chapter and locate children's unexplained experiences within different cultural contexts. Modern culture is technological, and children, digital natives. It's important therefore to examine children's unexplained experiences in cyberspace, considering how social media and virtual reality may initiate unexplained experiences in childhood.

Western Culture and Children's Unexplained Experiences

Children in the 21st century experience a very different world to those of earlier generations. Never has a generation had the freedoms to choose between many possible identities, experiences and opportunities. But they are also a generation that are losing connection to their cultural roots. In modern society, children are isolated from their adults, natural environments and indigenous stories. Institutional segregation of children from their families means that children spend most of their days in schools – and as adults, we lose connection with our children. Children and young people are starting to resist modern western culture in different ways. The emergence of "child activism", spearheaded by young people with concerns about the environment is one example. Recently in China, young people protested against appalling working conditions enforced on them. Chinese young people began to take a stand, by lying down on the ground, referred to as "Tang Ping".[28]

Resistance of younger children can be seen through their behaviors in school. Their unhappiness with strict regimes, testing and performing, manifests in what is clinically referred to as ADHD or behavioral disorders. Instead of examining the western systems that are counterintuitive to children's natural spontaneity, creativity and free nature, the child is considered dysfunctional. Modern social systems such as education and health are informed by a materialist paradigm rooted in physicalist science. The progression of technology and rise of neo-capitalist ideologies produces systems that sustain people as individual bio-machines. Schools behave as businesses that produce the next generation of compliant workers. But children, through their suffering, are resisting.

Just as there are two dominant narratives surrounding children's unexplained experiences, western society is infused with what Carol Merchant sees as two grand cultural narratives. The first is the biblical narrative of Christianity, the second the narrative of scientific revolution, both stories of recovery and progress that merged within the seventeenth century. Reason and experiment became the keys to reinventing a lost Eden, with explorations of the new world expanding capitalism and the rise of science and technology. Scientists saw the cosmos as a series of concentric spheres in motion, with the earth at the center. Humans were the object of all creation and the cosmos alive with a universal consciousness, with which people could interact and were influenced by. When Galileo declared that the Earth was not the center of the universe (nor humans), religious leaders issued orders for the torture or murder of any scientist who challenged the ideas of their faith. This saw a split between religion and science, reducing scientific enquiry to the nuts and bolts of how nature and the universe work. The idea of a universal consciousness was relegated to a personified version of God. What was lost in the demarcation of science from religion was the old wisdom or knowledge about nature, humans and the universe.

In the modern western world, there are sets of beliefs and values that define civilization and impose social order. Science and *modern* religion heavily influence western culture (and historically non-western cultures through colonization) that has resulted in a loss of ancient western knowledge. Raven Grimassi published a history of the "old religion" in 1999, in *The Wiccan Mysteries*. Grimassi's research draws on academic studies and oral histories that track movements of cultures, religions and spiritual practices across Europe. According to Grimassi, the history of "the old religion" extends back to the hunter-gathers' emergence into agricultural communities. When forest-dwelling humans began to form societies, their goddesses, gods and other ancient deities of the forest remained part of it. The Great Goddess was worshipped in the old European religious cultures, similar to the Earth Mother in Inca mythology. The mystery teachings were linked to women's cycles and childbirth, seeing men and women separated at these times. Men turned to form warrior-hunter cults, eventually challenging the structure of the matriarch descent and the value of its religious concepts. The image of the goddess/mother has been retained in modern patriarchal religious systems, for example, the Roman Catholic Church has Mary, mother of God. The roots of western modern religion are found in the old religion that saw communities of people living in harmony with the natural world and the universe.

The old religion of Europe was based on the laws of nature, its mystery tradition was a system through which people learn to "evolve spiritually through an understanding of the metaphysical laws reflected in the ways of nature."[29] Early humans made sense of the world through the forces of nature. Earthquakes and storms were attributed to the actions of a powerful agent. Personification of natural forces extended to spirits and other deities. The old teachings speak of legends of great gods who watched over them, with the early western shamans embodying rituals and practices to keep their communities safe. The philosophy of the old religion speaks of nature spirits called *elementals* or powerful protector entities known as the *watchers*. Behind the physical, according to the old religion, there are forces that animate the world known as air, earth, wind and fire, each having active agents (for example, earth is embodied through "gnomes"). Everything is created through these underlying forces and their agents – and everything is a manifestation of a divine consciousness where "souls experiencing the physical plane are like conscious probes sent out by the divine creator... or like brain cells in the mind of the divine creator."[30]

The old religion of Europe and its philosophy strongly corresponds with ancient Eastern religions such as Buddhism or Hinduism. Like the Eastern law of karma, the old religion of Europe refers to cause and effect and universal balance in similar terms. The cycles of birth and death and the aim to transcend them can also be found in Europe's old religion.[31] The roots of western culture appear to be consistent with the cultural myths and practices of First Nation communities across the world, as well as Eastern teachings. Many indigenous creation myths suggest the universe emerged from a thought or a mental process. The modern cultural narrative departs rapidly from its mystical roots. This is not surprising if we consider how people were killed for their beliefs.

Contemporary research into children's spirituality shows how children's experiences resonate with the Celtic connections among the human, natural and divine worlds.[32] Younger and older children in my own studies appear to experience phenomena that challenge modern western thought and resonate more with ancient paradigms. In the old tradition and medieval science, there is the idea of a universal consciousness that infuses human beings and nature. This is very different from modern cultural paradigm, which proposes an inert universe where humans are separate from the natural world. Children's experiences invite us to remember the lost wisdom of the old, through their resistance to western normative systems of thought.

Non-Western Cultures, Children and Unexplained Experiences

Until recent years, western scholars of anthropology examined the "exotic nature" of First Nation peoples, exploring rituals and practices that were very different to their own. Children were often missing from the journaled accounts of the customs and practices of indigenous communities.[33] This lack of concern with children in historical anthropology has resulted in little information about their ways of being and unexplained experiences. American anthropologist Edith Turner noted historical tensions when it came to the study of psi or unexplained experiences in First Nation settings. Western scholars made decisions about what could be included or excluded from the study of First Nation peoples. The scarcity of information about children's unexplained experiences in First Nation communities rests on western assumptions about the ritual and practices of indigenous peoples as savage or irrational. In post-colonial research, unexplained experiences of non-western young people are framed within biomedical or psychosocial models. Research with young people in non-western contexts shows a prevalence of unexplained experiences, linked to cultural factors such as "paranormal beliefs".[34] Instead of starting from the beliefs and practices of the culture of which the children are part, children's experiences are framed within western assumptions. Living experiences of the unseen are an important and everyday aspect of First Nation cultures and their religions. Children in some communities are encouraged to have certain types of experiences, such as conversing with deceased ancestors. Most cultural ideologies of First Nation communities privilege the unseen world, referred to as spirit. It follows that children's experiences of, for example, engaging with entities or hearing voices would be viewed as an everyday experience.

Children in First Nation contexts remain close to their cultural knowledges through practices such as oral storytelling, where folk tales are passed down through each generation. In the post-colonial world, First Nation children are exposed to multiple cultural narratives, through education and health systems. Research with Vietnamese American communities have shown how their beliefs are a mixture of biomedical models with narratives of magic.[35] For Vietnamese American communities, evil spirits and germs are thought to cause illness. Conceptions of childhood across the world influence how children's selves and experiences are understood. For example, the Beng community in West Africa believe that very young children know and understand everything that is said to them, even if in a language different to their own. The cultural narrative of the Beng people assumes a spirit world where children live before they are born, giving them access to a range of linguistic and cultural knowledge. The novelist Ben Okri wrote *The Famished Road*, an account of a Beng spirit child's journey between the spirit and earth world. In Beng tradition, a child remains in contact with the spirit world for several years and will decide to return if they are not cared for. Adults in fear of their children returning, treat them with great care and reverence.[36]

Elders have a mentorship role in their communities, teaching children about their cultural roots. Part of these teachings include how to navigate different realms of consciousness. A study of adolescent hallucinogenic plant ingestion, as part of the initiation rituals among young aboriginal males, Tsonga females and Chumash youth, by Grob & Dobkin,[37] found that young people were guided by elders. This meant their use of psychoactive substances were controlled and mentored by their elders. Any experiences are then theorized through indigenous knowledges. This is in sharp contrast with western adolescents who are not guided or supported when taking psychoactive substances, that can trigger expanded states and experiences. Studies on initiation rites in First Nation contexts show how elders in the community support and teach children and young people how to move thorough transitional phases. Not all ritual and initiation rites, known as *rites of passage*, are pleasant. There are reports of young people having to endure frightening and painful initiations, such as female circumcision. Some communities can use painful practices to induce altered states of consciousness, to commune with the gods, such as the dancers of the ritual sun dance of the Lakota Sioux. The dancers have wooden pegs inserted into their chest while attached by a cord to a central pole, the pain of the flesh wounds connecting the dancer with the sun father.[38]

Spirit dancing is practiced in many First Nation contexts. The Salish people in North America use spirit dancing as an initiation for young people who may be experiencing addiction to alcohol and drugs. The Salish community view this as spirit illness due to being separated from their own cultural heritage. The rationale for the spirit dance is to kill the old selves and rebirth into the path of the Salish tradition.[39] The initiation is long, involving three parts. Young people first enter a dark cubicle or smokehouse tent where they are subject to being restrained and physically attacked and tickled (an assault on the physical senses). Kinetic and acoustic stimulation is used (spun around, lifted, drums, rattles, singing), and these activities are repeated until the initiate is too weak to move. Physical training is the second stage of initiation with young people running long distances barefoot in snow, swimming in ice cold water and dancing. During this second stage, the spirit guardian will appear. The third phase involves teaching the young person the narratives and traditions of the community, where they are presented with new clothes that signify their new self. Young boys are often involved in rituals that can include fasting and staying alone in sacred places such as caves and mountains. The Ojibwa people use an initiation practice linked to puberty for boys who wish to become healers. The boys would be sent to a remote area to build a high platform in a tree with the task to lie there, waiting for a guardian spirit. The fasting and remoteness helped the young boys to enter a state of dissociated trance.[40] Boys reported consistent details of encounters with guardian spirits that mirrored stories of the Ojibway healers, suggesting how visions in altered states can fit a culturally prescribed pattern.[41]

The last examples show how experiences are induced in children by their community for the purposes of healing. Researching types of experiences with children in some cultural contexts can be a very dangerous act. I am referring to places where children (particularly orphans) suffer occult-based persecution, accused of witchcraft. Ally & Yew-Siong note how such practices occur predominantly in African countries.[42] Religio-cultural abuse of children can be located within historical Christian cultures too, where believers equated children's misbehavior with the activities of Satan or other evil spirits. The European witch trials saw many children accused of witchcraft, seen as having too much knowledge about black magic (seen as a strong affiliation with nature). It was often parents who accused their children of witchcraft because children engaged in activities such as rough play or sexual behavior.

Research, Children's Unexplained Experiences and Culture

Recent times have seen more ethical research practices *with* indigenous communities. Strict international research protocols, and the changing hearts and minds of researchers, have resulted in better research practice *with* indigenous communities based on participation, respect and honesty. Natalie Tobert is one such researcher who published "Cultural

Perspectives on Mental Wellbeing" in 2017. Tobert aims to explore any parallels between mental well-being, spiritual awakening and unexplained experiences, considering how experiences are thought of as on a continuum from normal, to anomalous to abnormal. Tobert provides examples of how distressing unexplained experiences may be interpreted by people from different cultures. Somali residents in London used different ways to address their suffering, such as attending mosques to have healing passages from the Koran read onto them. Stigma prevented them from accessing mainstream services. Tobert goes on to explain how a high number of Somali people were being diagnosed with schizophrenia – 92% out of 32 people. This appears to be statistically unlikely and raised the issue of not listening to people's historical and cultural narratives in diagnostic procedures. The anthropological studies Tobert conducted with psychiatrists, clairvoyants and religious leaders in India found many reasons for difficult experiences. For example, misbehavior can result in the wrath of the deities or the land spirit entities (those who have not incarnated and those who have).

Data from my own studies suggest how cultural explanations of unexplained experiences (both positive and negative) can affect how children are supported by their families and communities. For example, a young person of Indian heritage, living in the UK, was suffering through repetitive thoughts, visions and voice-hearing. The young person's family suggested they were cursed, possessed by evil spirits. The young person was taken to an elder in the community who read passages from the Koran and gave the parents special herbs to give to their child. However, the young person's peers advised that his experiences were symptomatic of mental illness. These two worldviews created inner conflict for the young person, torn between two cultures. This is very common for children and young people living in western countries, in communities that retain their religious and cultural values. I recently spoke with a young person from the Hindu community. Feeling lost and depressed, he reported that his knowledge about the ancient scriptures of his religion supported his difficult experiences. The concept of *atman* or belief that the soul is part of a supreme soul in this young person's belief system meant that his limitations could be overcome. There was hope. Belief is very different from living experience, and this young person found those experiences through practices of yoga and meditation – practices deeply intertwined within his own cultural framework. The conflict was still there for this young person despite his self-gnosis, catalyzed by teachers and peers who view the self and world in very different ways.

Spiritual Emergencies and Children

Spiritual emergency was coined by Stanislav and Christina Grof in the early nineties to describe a crisis "that can occur spontaneously without any precipitating factors", triggered by emotional stress, disease, accidents, childbirth and other events.[43] Spiritual emergencies can be very distressing for people and often mistaken for psychosis. The outcome for spiritual emergency can be "the movement of an individual to a more expanded way of being that involves enhanced emotional and psychosomatic health, greater freedom of personal choices and a sense of deeper connection with other people, nature and the cosmos."[44] Knowledge about spiritual emergency has grown through social media and movements such as Emerging Proud in the UK or Mad in America in the US. Survivor movements are made up of adults who have suffered within the mainstream mental health system, and resist diagnosis and medicalization of their experiences. In an article published by Mick Collins (et al) in 2010, the authors suggest that a current global crisis is catalyzing in adults a collective shift in consciousness. The authors argue how spiritual emergencies as a transformational phenomena may be revealing spontaneous changes in consciousness, that could lead people to experience greater depths in the way that they live.

I would suggest that a similar process is happening among children. Although children are not often included in literature around spiritual emergency and transformation, their experiences are very similar to those used to describe adults' unexplained experiences, emergencies and transformation. I have seen examples of young people in my own research that appear to have a spontaneous crisis, followed by transformation and continuous well-being. In younger children, these transitional states can be seen at different stages of their individual and collective growth and development (as children vary at when they move through different stages of development). They can often be referred to as a growth-spurt that can bring feelings of unsettlement, an increase in nightmares and night terrors or feelings of social anxiety. These aspects of younger children's transitional states can be quickly medicalized in western societies. The physicalist scientific paradigm that has become the west's go-to narrative, does not include traditional cultural knowledge that has been lost in the mire of progression.

New Technologies and Children's Unexplained Experiences

The appeal for children and young people to the supernatural may be influenced through a need to reclaim lost knowledge. The film and video game industries tap into children's curiosities, producing gods and demons, heavens and hells for children to explore and immerse in. Archetypal figures and realities emerge through the communal storytelling of online communities, much like those practices found in the oral storytelling of ancient and indigenous peoples. Vivian Asimos uses the "Slenderman" as an example of a thoughtform given life, whose mythology is connected to paranormal narratives such as *the black-eyed children*. Young users are immersed between play and non-play online, with the boundaries between fantasy and reality collapsed. For example, a typical rule on forums where Slenderman can be found is *everything is true here even if it isn't*. As users play with the concept of truth and belief, many children report anxieties around tulpas (thoughtforms that carry power) such as the Slenderman, with the boundaries between the virtual and physical worlds of children disrupted. At the same time, online contexts offer children freedoms to share and express their own interests and experiences of the unexplained. In a space where fantasy, fact and freedom are available.

Children aged between 7-18 years spend a large amount of time in cyberspace. The most prolific users are children aged 8-12 years. Modern children are digital natives, with technology playing a prominent role in identity formation and their relational experiences with others and the world. Children as young as two years are tech-savvy with the introduction of iPads into day-care settings and nursery schools. Electronic literacies form a large part of educational and everyday activity for children across a wide cultural, social and age range. Video gaming is a genre of online engagement that is hugely popular with tweens and teens. A recent article[45] reports the findings from a large European online study with 25,000 children aged 9-16 years, that examined their video gaming habits. The data shows how 83% of children find enjoyment from playing video games in online environments. Children globally are immersing themselves in cyberspace, transcending their normal physical-geographical boundaries. Two recent studies in the USA found that 90-95% of American teens use social media on a regular basis. A recent study in the UK examined the usage of children on sites such as TikTok, concluding that children can move effectively between the public and the private – challenging adults' perceptions that they are vulnerable online. The downside of children's online activity is its potential addictive nature, with some scholars suggesting that young people can become addicted to the Internet, demonstrating withdrawal symptoms such as aggression or restlessness.[46]

The association between enhanced cognitive skills and video game play has been well documented. Video gaming is seen as an amplifier, like meditation or prayer, that can catalyze "higher levels of consciousness".[47] A correspondence between a high prevalence of lucid dreaming and video game playing was found in studies in the early 2000s.[48] Virtual reality landscapes found in video gaming can induce cognitive enhancement in children such as spatial visualization, perceptual speed, ability to reason metacognitively and reflective decision-making. These are cognitive perceptions found in unexplained experiences of children, especially those that report OBEs, lucid and exceptional dreams and peak experiences. There appears to be a correlation between children's online living experiences with a rise of self-reporting of unexplained experiences. Rather than *psychological absorption*, as suggested by some scholars,[49] perhaps children's frequent absorption into online activities amplifies or makes clear, experiences considered as unexplained.

In recent times, VR has been used as a site for learning and rehearsal, using virtual landscapes to practice responses in *real* social settings. VR is viewed by some professionals as a positive learning aid for children with autism who can struggle immensely in social settings, especially school.[50] VR learning is a similar process one can undertake in lucid dream states where professional athletes are known to train to enable them to practice their sport in sleeping hours.[51] Virtual environments can facilitate wheelchair users to experience the world from a standing perspective.[52] Aisha (from chapter 1) as a wheelchair user experienced through an OBE (or "strange experience" in Aisha's words) the world from a standing perspective. These similarities in experience between VR users, lucid dreamers and OBErs, may hold clues to the nature of everyday reality as similar with our dream states. Children's unexplained and online worlds could begin to shed more light on the nature of reality.

Children's Unexplained Experiences and Cyberspace

For children, cyberspace offers a way to share their fascination and experiences of the unexplained in late modernity. The lost knowledge of the western world sees a deficit for children in locating their experiences and making sense of them. Online contexts provide opportunities for children to channel their interests, experiences and knowledge, from a cyber identity, an avatar – different from the everyday roles that children are expected to play. Access to information and affordances to participate in topics viewed as taboo in school settings, for example, have made cyberspace a rich site for children's reporting of unexplained experiences. Communication in cyberspace transcends normal conventions of the written word. The fluid, speed and range of sensory stimuli allows children to convey experiences in a similar way that art and mark making can. For a researcher, cyberspace provides a rich site for exploration into children's unexplained experiences, providing the ethical conditions are in place. This is more important when there are a wealth of unethical activities taking place online, not so much with children, more from parents of younger children.

There are many examples of parents putting revealing photographs and videos online of their small children. These often go viral with little protections for the young child who features in the images. Recent examples include a child aged around three years old. The parents have captured on video the toddler becoming frightened by something under the bed. The child is alone in the bedroom with a remote camera capturing how the child appears to be dragged under the bed by a mysterious force. What is disturbing about this video is the authentic and emotional reaction from the child and her movements as she disappears under the bed. This is one example of content that is currently distributed across online sites. There are many examples of adults sharing their children's unexplained experiences, such as reports of past life memories, having visions or premonitions, on sites such as Twitter. Adults can report their own unexplained experiences from childhood too. It seems that social media offers a freedom to share experiences that cannot be expressed in mainstream or physical contexts.

#OurUnusualExperiences

It seems children in cyberspace access nonphysical realities that intersect with their material lives. Since 2018, I have been observing unexplained experiences of children online. The psychic child narrative pervades cyberspace, in the forms of paranormal movies, urban legends and songs. In indigenous settings, there are spaces and space holders (such as elders) for transitional and unexplained experiences – in cyberspace there are no guides or mentors to support children. Unexplained experiences and interests are abundant in cyberspace as it provides a liberating (albeit more troublesome) space for children. Children's unexplained experiences are reported in different ways online, and their strategies depend on the platform being used. Children can share their own experiences, often reporting shadow people, poltergeist activity and exceptional dreams. Young people conduct their own experiments and record them, such as ghost hunts in remote places, mirror and glass experiments and necrophonic applications (spirit box applications etc.).

There are thousands of reports from children and adults about unexplained experiences online; some appear authentic while many do not (parodies, jokes, hyperbole etc.). These are experiences that transcend cultural differences but are often framed in supernatural narratives – as the only model available. Children who may not have naturally occurring experiences are seeking them out through different types of experiments. I've highlighted the dangers of this in chapter 1, yet these practices seem to show a need for children to explore the unseen. If children's material worlds are tightly governed by certain cultural practices, cyberspace offers freedoms to shape their identities and beliefs that contest adult perspectives. As shown through the chapter, cultural beliefs and practices really do influence children's unexplained experiences – in positive or negative ways.

When experiences are fundamental to the cultural narrative, for example in First Nation contexts where value is placed in the unseen worlds, children are supported and guided. First Nation people retain their ancient wisdom through ritual, storytelling and cultural practices. Western culture seems to have lost touch with the original wisdom, its narrative now consistent with a material view of the world, making experiences of children in the west impossible. Materialism implies that matter is the only substance, and everything that is a fact is dependent on physical causes (see later chapters for further discussion). This includes the mind and our very selves. Children challenge this view of reality, through their unexplained experiences and ways of being. As well as losing touch with the old wisdom, the study of unexplained experiences in the west has been ruptured through the emergence of the grand narrative of mental health. In the next chapter, I examine a history of unexplained experiences in childhood.

Chapter 3

A History of Unexplained Experiences in Childhood

In the 1960s, parapsychologist Louisa Rhine collected over 30,000 letters sent by adults who had unexplained experiences. Among these letters were 216 contributions from children aged between 10-18 years. Rhine handpicked and examined children's letters that reported unexplained experiences, looking for spontaneous psi experiences, such as precognition and intuitive experiences.[53] Analysis of paranormal experiences were performed on the letters of children, using a chi-square method. This is when different hypotheses are tested against each other about a certain claim (i.e., children are telepathic). The chi-square helps to know if experiences exceed random chance, and the data will match one of the presented hypotheses (statements of truth to be tested). The results from Rhine's analysis showed how children's precognitive dreams were about themselves and pets, with trivial events scoring higher than more serious events such as injury or death. Rhine's interests in children (and the elderly) ensured that they were included (even in a small way) into studies that examined unexplained experiences. As Athena Drewes writes in an article published in 2002,[54] "some critics contend that because these letters were not independently verified or validated, they cannot account for proof of ESP phenomena." Such attitudes still prevail in unexplained experience scholarship today, discounting the value of examining these experiences in everyday contexts and the natural world.

Past experiments with children yield some interesting conclusions that could be used to support how children's unexplained experiences could be understood now. In this chapter, I include some historical studies and discuss some of the issues raised by including children in scientific experiments. I also consider the potential value for these approaches and findings. Research methods such as chi-squares and hypotheses are aiming for knowledge through objectivity. These are ways of doing research that come from physicalist science, used to test claims about truth and correlations between things, for example, mind and matter. The letters sent by children in the example above are subjective data. There is a simple disjunct between using objective measurement methods to test the validity of subjective human experience – but we must not throw the proverbial baby out with the bathwater. Studies that aim to show how the mind can influence matter are important. The wealth of scientific literature on psi experiences and adults appears to be more robust than conventional psychological studies. Parapsychologists need to work harder to evidence their hypotheses and this shows through their empirical and experimental endeavors. In this chapter, I consider children's unexplained experiences from a psi perspective, locating children's experiences in the parapsychology field. There are many valuable findings from past studies that could inform a fresh way to think about children's unexplained experiences.

Young Frauds

On the other end of the spectrum are claims about children's unexplained experiences that may be based on a combination of flawed evidence and mischievous children. Arthur Conan Doyle, the author famous for creating Sherlock Holmes, became interested in the paranormal, searching for ways to capture evidence of different realities. In his book *The Coming of the Fairies*, published in 1922, Conan Doyle presented the (now famous) case of the Cottingley Fairies. Conan Doyle in the opening of the book proposed the photographs as "either the most elaborate and ingenious hoax ever played upon the public or else they constitute an event in human history which may in the future appear to have been epoch-making in its character". Two young girls,

Frances and Elsie, had taken alleged photographs of fairies in the garden of their idyllic home in the South of England. For years, people pondered over the authenticity of the photographs, with Conan Doyle himself not quite convinced the pictures were fake. I remember as a little girl having my own beliefs crushed about the Cottingley fairies, when in 1983 Frances and Elsie confessed the whole thing had been fake – 50 years after Conan Doyle's book. Skeptic researcher James Randi debunked the fairies when he noted how the fairy characters strongly resembled figures in children's books published in 1911. Randi further exposed discrepancies in the exposure of the photographs, pointing out the image of the waterfall behind the fairies that didn't quite match the pristine stillness of the fairies' wings:

A. FRANCES AND THE FAIRIES.

Photograph taken by Elsie. Bright sunny day in July 1917. The "Midg" camera. Distance, 4 ft. Time, 1/50ᵗʰ sec. The original negative is asserted by expert photographers to bear not the slightest trace of combination work, retouching, or anything whatever to mark it as other than a perfectly straight single-exposure photograph, taken in the open air under natural conditions. The negative is sufficiently, indeed somewhat over-exposed. The waterfall and rocks are about 20 ft. behind Frances, who is standing against the bank of the beck. A fifth fairy may be seen between and behind the two on the right. The colouring of the fairies is described by the girls as being of very pale pink, green, lavender, and mauve, most marked in the wings and fading to almost pure white in the limbs and drapery. Each fairy has its own special colour.

[Page 31

Image 2: The Cottingley Fairies, July 1917

As Elsie explained in a TV interview in 1983, it was people's need to believe in magic that kept the debate alive. James Randi was very good at identifying children's skullduggery in scientific experiments, exposing quite a few inauthentic cases in his long and influential career. However, his work may have had some detrimental consequences for children who are not faking their experiences. Randi shows how easy children can manipulate experiments for fun. Experiments use specialized practices and languages that are not of much interest within the lifeworlds of children – unless they are doing the experimenting!

I know from experience what can happen when children become bored in research studies. But this doesn't mean that children have no capacities to be active research subjects and agents in research that examines unexplained experiences. Stanley Krippner brings attention to the possibilities of fraud when designing studies with children, recognizing how psychic experiences will intersect with moods, physical states and motivation of the child. What may affect experimental studies with children more is the similarity between performance-related tasks undertaken in school and psi experiments. Educational languages, practices and environments evoke unspoken expectations on children. Children are expected to behave obediently, perform well and attain positive results. Power relationships between teachers and children (even in the case of sweet teachers) determine how children think and feel when conducting tests.

Historical Research into Children's Unexplained Experiences

In 1943, AA Foster conducted an experiment with "50 children attending a government school for Plains-Indians in Canada who were given tests for ESP from a white teacher."[55] In the last chapter, I highlighted the issues for First Nation children in government run schools. The experiment detailed by Foster would be problematic for children in these settings if the wider context is not considered. A

51

recent history of research into children's unexplained experiences can be found in parapsychology literature that starts around the 1950s and seems to dwindle in early 2000. The reframing of children's unexplained experiences into dominant mental health narratives may account for this apparent rupture in these types of studies. The literature seems to take two directions with children's unexplained experiences. There is a body of literature that examines children's *mystical experiences*, modelled from Maslow's self-actualization theories; and a body of literature concerned with scientific experiments of children's psi abilities, such as PK (telekinesis, telepathy and premonitions).

Mystical experiences were (and are still) explained in terms of spirituality, where children experience a union with a greater force than themselves, often triggered in natural environments or (as my own studies show) following intense periods of suffering. In 1965, Bindl found that numinous or mystical experiences were common in children under seven years, becoming less frequent in older children. Mystical or religious experiences are shown to be common by Alister Hardy in his research study of 1000 children and young people. While Ed Hoffman's book *Visions of Innocence*, published in the early nineties, contains narrative accounts of children's mystical experiences. Robinson and Hoffman found that these types of experiences would occur in children as young as three years. In a recent talk, a questioner asked me, "What is the youngest age that you have recorded a mystical experience?" I tried to explain that it is difficult to record these types of experiences in younger children as they appear to already "be there". In other words, there seems to be a natural union with others and the world. Older children have developed layers of conditioned beliefs and a stronger sense of personhood. When older children have a peak or mystical experience, they are more aware of moving outside the boundaries of a seemingly separate self so can reflect on this process. There is a large body of contemporary literature that examines mystical experiences of children under the umbrella of *children's spirituality*. Children's mystical experiences are largely examined within narratives of religiosity, within contexts of education, that may not offer a naturalistic view of children's experiences.

Athena Drewes has been researching children's unexplained experiences since the early 1980s and supports children through play-centered therapy work. With Sally Ann Drucker, Drewes compiled an anthology of children's paranormal experiences in the 1990s, bringing together a compilation of studies, including their own research. In a 1997 article, Drewes brought attention to how parapsychology overlooks children and claims that children are easier to research paranormal experiences with than adults. Drewes suggests that children have not yet accepted cultural concepts regarding what is possible or impossible, nor are children negatively conditioned about psychic phenomena. In modern times, children (from a younger age) are consistently bombarded with negative content around paranormal phenomena, as discussed in previous chapters. Drewes makes some interesting observations about children's limited concept of time, space and force (more so younger children) and highlights the need to adapt experimental conditions to meet the needs and interests of the child. Sadly, at times children appear to be unknowingly subjugated in historical research. For example, statements such as *"children who are obedient will present few problems"*[56] are extremely problematic, ethically and for the findings. Research that positions children as active agents is more likely to generate more accurate findings, as children relax into experiments or research activities in more natural ways.

Babies and Psi

It may be difficult to imagine how we can research with babies. Scholars of childhood studies have developed theories and methods to undertake research that explores the experiences of babies. Infants, in some social science studies, are viewed as non-separate from their environment. In this way, babies are understood as an assemblage of all the other things, within their environment. This means, all the external *material* context surrounding the baby will account for an analysis of baby and his experiences. Child psychologist Suzanne Zeedyk asks, "How does the infant brain provide insight into spiritual experiences?" Zeedyk suggests that babies arrive already connected and can reveal our natural human connectedness – seen through babies' facial expressions, eye movements and interactions with caregivers. Scholars who study babies include the sounds that babies make and their movements as rich research data. Babies were also included in historical studies of psi experiences – but these studies appear to be sparse. In the early fifties, scientists such as Fisk and Bierman worked with infants aged 10-14 months to test PK or telekinesis and clairvoyance. While Braud, in the early eighties, tested babies aged 6 weeks-12 months old. The studies involved using computer-generated video displays of a laughing face display and melody. Braud's tests also involved playback of their mother's voices. While Fisk obtained significant clairvoyance results with a 14-month-old infant, results from other studies proved to be inconclusive.

Studies have focused more on the symbiotic relationship between mothers and babies, and how children can be particularly receptive to other people's feelings. In her book, *The Mother Link: Stories of Psychic Bonds between Mother and Child,* Cassandra Eason analyses maternal telepathy between mothers and babies. Eason suggests that the bonds between mothers and their children start before birth and extend after death. Experiences of ESP (extrasensory phenomena) in children have been theorized as extensions of our natural perceptual processes by parapsychologists who have studied children. In the early seventies, parapsychologist Jan Ehrenwald, theorized telepathy as the embryological matrix of communication between mother and child – where telepathic communication takes place when the child is in utero. Psychiatrist Stanislav Grof also concluded how babies-in-utero communicate telepathically with their mothers. Grof's "peri-natal matrix" model was developed through research with thousands of adults who were regressed back into utero through psychotropic experimental methods (see chapter 8 for a fuller discussion). Preverbal children are highly dependent on their mother's care and may exhibit a natural telepathic mode of communication.

Ehrenwald suggested that psi experiences such as telepathy become more repressed as children become older; they are substituted by *normal* perceptual and motor processes. For example, telepathy and clairvoyance would be extensions of normal perceptual processes, precognition the reverse of memory and PK an extension of motor abilities in younger children. These observations point to psi phenomena as natural human experiences that we may have lost touch with. Perhaps they are always there yet we are not conscious of them in the business of the adult-world. Past studies focus on younger children, yet in my recent studies, a high incidence of teenagers report feeling others' emotions, bodily sensations and knowing what they are thinking. To a point where it can be overwhelming for these young people. It could be that older children are reclaiming lost modes of communication and connection. This raises questions about why older children are becoming more conscious of using extended cognitive abilities, naturally used by infants. Rather than regression, as proposed by earlier researchers to explain adult psi, it may suggest an evolutionary momentum as our current systems and ways of thinking are breaking down.

Psi and School-Aged Children

In 1957, Rhine & Pratt in their book *Parapsychology: Frontier Science of the Mind* suggest that schools may be a natural testing site for the study of ESP. In an article from 1972, John Randall noted how research with children and psi experiences had been sparse, except for a handful of studies conducted in America and Europe. In the 1950s school experiments were recorded in Holland by Van Busschbach, and in the US by Anderson & White. In the early 1960s, Anderson & White ran experiments that explored whether a positive teacher-student relationship would affect ESP scores. The authors concluded after three separate experiments, that is does.[57] Beloff & Bate, in the early seventies, conducted psi experiments with schoolchildren in Scotland, with significant results. Past studies in schools have been successful in showing how children perform ESP related tasks. Studies were undertaken using different types of psi experiments with children. Adult experiments were adapted to suit the interests and understandings of school-aged children such as replacing traditional psi card symbols with pictures of animals.[58] Younger students scored higher than older students on clairvoyance, PK and precognitive tasks. Research, carried out in the early eighties with children from Mexico, found that clairvoyance and precognition scores correlated negatively with abilities in math, how long children had been in school and age of participants. In the eighties, Susan Blackmore attempted to correlate ESP and personal variables such as attitudes and/or beliefs, competition and cooperation, advancing experiments with children, through including other contextual factors. Schools may provide an ideal site for conducting psi experiments with children. There are lots of children in school, already engaging in tests and measurement activities. However, there are many factors that may influence how children perform in psi studies in school contexts. I know from researching in educational contexts for several years that children respond, behave and engage in school-based research in ways that are different from their natural environments.

In 2005, Christian Hallman wanted to study intuition in

children and carried out an experiment with 2,040 children in a school environment, using computer software. The software would measure the intuitive ability of predicting a future randomly selected target. The test was thirty trials, with comparators used such as gender and age. The findings show how females and younger children perform precognitive tasks more than males and older age groups – with the only highly significant finding found in children aged 3-6 years of age. This result may correspond with theories of younger children as more naturally utilizing our natural modes of communication such as telepathy or "memory-reversal" (precognition). School expects children to have linguistic capital, modes of communication that are valued. Younger children may default into their preverbal modes in contexts which demand the acquisition of new ways of expression.

Intuition is not understood by science and is defined as the ability for obtaining immediate or direct knowledge. Research by Bowers et al in the early nineties concluded that intuition guided students to accurately guess the correct solutions in tasks, despite being uncertain of coherent patterns during verbal and nonverbal tasks.[59] Hallman notes that intuition may also be linked to creativity, "having a physiological interface with the heart, pineal body and right cerebral hemispheres."[60] Past studies I have conducted with teachers in classrooms that considered the best ways to teach and learn, showed interventions using music and art in science lessons increased attainment levels in students' science tests. It seems psi abilities can be taught to children. Between 2012-2015, Chuang Chung and Tai-Chun Yang improved the abilities of Taiwanese blind children to see and read through skin contact. The children demonstrated skin reading colors, numbers and figures on cards. In some cases, 100% accuracy of readings were recorded. The children were also taught to communicate telepathically. In similar studies by Chuang Chung, sighted children were taught PK abilities, to fold strips of paper held within transparent sealed containers. Are children in these cases learning something new or are children remembering their natural capacities as human beings?

Children's Unexplained Experiences, Creativity and Well-Being

Alex Tanous was a renowned parapsychologist and philosopher who published a book with KF Donnelly in 1979, entitled *Is Your Child Psychic: A Guide for Creative Parents and Teachers*. In the last chapter, I looked at the problems with labelling children as either psychic or non-psychic. However, the ethos of Tanous & Donnelly's book fits more with the naturalistic perspective of unexplained experiences (they are a natural part of being human) rather than with a narrative of giftedness. Tanous & Donnelly explain the brain as a radio receiver rather than a producer of the mind, starting from the idea that children who have unexplained experiences are *tuning in* to other aspects of reality. The book is intended to guide adults who support children and their unexplained experiences as the authors know *"that children suffer their own private hells"*. Sound advice is offered by Tanous & Donnelly as they provide a list of simple experiments that adults can do with children. These activities are framed by CPE – Creative Perceptive Energy, and the authors encourage adults to facilitate children's innate psychic experiences in a creative manner for their children's well-being.

Tanous & Donnelly point to the potential healing capabilities of children's unexplained experiences if they are responded to in meaningful ways by adults. The authors' observations are similar to the findings I published in 2021, in an article that shows how children who have positive and negative unexplained experiences all reported healing and growth from them. This included spontaneously giving up antidepressant medication (for older children), knowing we are more than our bodies, feeling connected to the world and so on. How we frame and understand children's unexplained experiences has important consequences for their well-being.

Tanous & Donnelly include in their book a range of unexplained experiences in different contexts, differing from the traditional focus on psi abilities, experimental studies and tricky contexts such as schools. According to the authors, children can perceive mood through colors and detect illness in others. How adults respond to children's unexplained experiences are also included – an important facet of these types of studies – and an issue that is consistently identified by children in the studies I undertake. Imaginary playmates are discussed by Tanous & Donnelly, and they caution adults to respond to children's reports in careful ways. Five categories of imaginary playmates are identified by the authors (with some word changes):

1. "Real" playmates – engaged with through the usual perceptions of sight, sound, smell, touch
2. Telepathic communication – with an invisible playmate
3. Spirit communication – with a deceased or otherworldly being
4. Duplication of the child – dual consciousness where the child's consciousness produces a second version of the child
5. Out of body experiences or bi-location

These categories of imaginary playmates seem to correspond with different states of consciousness. For example, playmates children engage with in everyday waking states and some experiences, such as out of body, may occur in hypnogogic states – the state between sleep and waking. I have not yet come across many children who report imaginary friends (only my own daughter when she was very young) but have heard accounts of children (younger and older) engaging with beings. Some may be frightening, described as "tall with no faces" or "like a dog with red eyes". These can be one-off meetings or repeated occurrences. Such as a young child who reported nightly occurrences of a shape-shifting entity that would visit him. Children seem to take these experiences with more ease than adults. The way children can present these experiences as matter of fact, while shrugging their shoulders and waiting for more exciting things to do (such as getting into my research toolbox that contains toys, paints and other thrilling paraphernalia), suggests they are a normal aspect of their lives. Tanous & Donnelly highlight how children know the difference between a playmate conjured through their imaginations and playmates that may correspond to one of the categories they offer.

Learning from the Past

Past studies focus extensively on psi in children, examining extrasensory phenomena and the effect of mind on matter. If you now search "psi and children" you will find that psi's meaning has morphed into "Parenting Stress Index"! There is a sense that many experiments with children were not continued by scholars in the field. This may be due to inconclusive findings, difficulties involving children in traditional experiments and advances in other scholarship (i.e., psychology, health and childhood studies). A return to exploring unexplained experiences in childhood is important, providing it can involve different ways and a more inclusive ethos for engaging children in these types of studies. Studying children's unexplained experiences needs to account for the metaphysical assumptions and sociocultural influences that intersect with how children experience self, others and the world. Historically and in contemporary research, this way of studying subjective experience is still privileged for generating knowledge about the way things *really are*. Sometimes measures such as statistics and modelling can get in the way of good qualitative studies, and other times can enhance them. Nevertheless, combining different approaches to research such as experiment data, with how everyday people ascribe meanings to their living experiences, can only enhance our understanding of human experience. Regardless of how much attention to methodological procedures researchers give, we cannot always be prepared for how children will engage with the research.

There are important findings from studies of the past that can inform how children's unexplained experiences are understood in contemporary society. Past research shows a range of experiences that challenge mainstream views about reality and the relationship between mind and matter. How scholars of the past theorize psi experiences as extensions of our normal human cognition has potential for reauthoring and re-understanding children's unexplained experiences. Studies have shown how younger children are more likely to show cognitive capacities such as telepathy and precognition, perhaps compensating when the world demands linguistic skills. Through examining imaginary friends, Tanous & Donnelly move unexplained experiences towards altered states of consciousness through ideas such as "dual consciousness". Past studies show how children's experiences can violate our normative ideas of space-time. Similarly, present studies by renowned scholars in the fields of psychology, neuroscience and child psychiatry also challenge mainstream ideas through children's experiences. These studies are discussed in the next chapter.

Chapter 4

New Studies in Unexplained Experiences in Childhood

Scientific research on unexplained experiences in childhood is sparse, historically and within contemporary academia. One exception is the work of Ian Stevenson who extensively studied children and reincarnation before his death in 2007. Dr. Stevenson's work has been continued by Jim Tucker, based at the University of Virginia's Perceptual Studies Unit. I discuss Tucker's continuing research on past life memories of children in this chapter. Contemporary research involving children and unexplained experiences such as telepathy and near-death experiences are also included. The work of prominent scientists and researchers in the fields of psychology, neuroscience and near-death studies are examined to develop an understanding of unexplained experiences in childhood.

Validating Telepathy in Children

In 1959, Soal & Bowden published *The Mind Readers: Some Recent Experiments in Telepathy*, a book that described a series of psi experiments run with two young Welsh boys. The boys were first cousins and demonstrated highly significant clairvoyant results across tests. One of the boys also showed successful results when working with other agents. The experiments caused debates from scholars of the time that appeared in the *British Journal of Psychology* in the early sixties, notably between Sir Cyril Burt and CEM Hansel – who criticized Sir Burt's claims that the experiments may be evidence of telepathy. Stanley Krippner describes telepathy as one manifestation of the collective phenomena of ESP (extrasensory perception), involving information received by a subject from an agent, through some type of mind-to-mind contact.[61] Carl Jung vouched for the authenticity of telepathy, not as a paranormal or exceptional skill, but as a natural part of our human experience that we cannot always access.[62] In my own research with children, many report experiences of hearing other people's thoughts. As is the case in qualitative research practice, when an experience is reported consistently across individuals or groups of people, the phenomenon will be considered valid. As there are very little qualitative studies that examine unexplained experiences in childhood, these types of experiences have not been recorded extensively in children. One of the difficulties in convincing others about the validity of children's experiences of telepathy, is the lack of evidence; for example, having tangible proof that a child is reading the mind of another person. Why would it be necessary to evidence an experience such as telepathy? Children can feel distressed by intrusive thoughts, which don't quite feel like their own. If children had an understanding that thoughts may be part of a larger field of mind, perhaps they might not be so distressed or feel shameful, by believing they are generating unpleasant thoughts (see chapter 8 for an extended discussion of children and intrusive thoughts).

Diane Hennacy Powell, a neuropsychiatrist and author of *The ESP Enigma*, is conducting research that is starting to show evidence for telepathy in children with savant autism. Savant syndrome is viewed as a condition in which people with certain disabilities and developmental issues, such as severe autism, demonstrate extraordinary skill that stands in stark contrast to how they function in other areas (such as socializing, speech, motor skills etc.). Approximately one in 10 people with autism has some savant skills. In other forms of developmental disability, savant skills occur in less than 1% of people. Around 75% of persons with savant syndrome have been diagnosed with autism while 25% have some other form of developmental disability.[63] Powell has conducted case study research with a small number of children who are identified with savant autism.

Between 2013-2018, Powell carried out home-testing with three children in the USA, under controlled conditions. In these experiments, randomized words, letters, numbers and pictures were used to assess whether these children were actively accessing the mind of the reader (the target reading the random symbols). The children demonstrated astounding accuracy during these experiments. This led Powell to conduct a formal study with one child, using numerous controlled sessions. The child was asked to read the therapist's mind. The therapist was asked to write verbal descriptions of the images that could be compared to the child's answers, which were registered by means of a pointer and letter stencil. In addition, random numbers were generated for mathematical equations. The experiment used time-synchronized and time-stamped cameras, as well as several microphones. The child achieved incredible hit rates, sometimes 100% accuracy with images that contained up to 9 letters. This was the same for number equations. Powell aims to continue these studies using quantitative electroencephalography (to monitor activity in the brain during ESP activity).

Powell suggests that such abilities in autistic children support the idea that savant skills are a manifestation of underlying psi ability. Nonverbal children may use telepathy as a default communication strategy that emerges through a strong desire to communicate with their caregivers. Powell's important research could support how we understand the nature of mind and how children in distress, younger children and children with medical conditions, access latent capacities to communicate for socialization and survival. Some of the children I research with have medical conditions (such as epilepsy, narcolepsy, cerebral palsy, autism spectrum), and some do not. In a small pilot study, I conducted with a sample of 16 children, I examined whether children with medical conditions had different types of unexplained experiences (such as a higher incidence of telepathy) than children with no medical conditions.

The simple table (see Table 1) shows that regardless of their health status, children (aged 4-18 years) have the same types of experiences.

Table 1: Pre-existing and no pre-existing medical conditions and unexplained experiences

Epilepsy	Voice-hearing, premonitions, peak/transformational experiences, lucid dreams, speaking with deceased relatives, telepathy, sense of being stared at
Narcolepsy with Cataplexy	Visions, engaging with unseen beings, telepathy, premonitions, sense of being stared at, lucid dreams
Hospitalization for short-term conditions	NDE, peak/transformational experiences, visions, engaging with unseen beings, sense of being stared at
No medical conditions (long or short term)	Voice-hearing, premonitions, telepathy, lucid dreams, out of body experiences, peak/transformational experiences, engaging with unseen beings, sense of being stared at

This example is based on a very small sample size and the data was collated through multiple individual research sessions with children. It's also important to note that these studies are ongoing to enable more children to be involved, across different cultural contexts. The table is useful to show how these experiences are not always determined by a medical condition. In this study, children reported telepathy within their close networks (parents, carers and peers), suggesting that telepathy is a normal mode of socialization when we share close bonds with others.

Children and Experiments

Powell's ground-breaking research with children will prove valuable for understanding the nature of mind and our latent capabilities as human beings. It is important when involving children in traditional research studies that we are still critical of any underlying assumptions about the children and phenomena being investigated. For example, it is unclear what autism *is*. Autism is viewed as a medical condition that is identified through clinical diagnostics based on how children experience self, others and the world. Wendy Chung, a scientist at the Simons Foundation, in her recent TED talk, "Autism – what we know (and what we don't know yet)"[64] explains how no one really knows what causes autism. Scientists will define autism through different lenses, for example social or genetic. What is evident in Chung's talk is that there is no consensus about what autism *is*, despite its status as a matter-of-fact condition. In 2006, William Stillman published *Autism and the God Connection*, a book that aims to redefine the autistic experience. Stillman includes autobiographical material and accounts of the children he supports in his role as a counsellor. Stillman shares the story of Boone, a five-year-old boy with autism. Boone's mother reported that six months prior to the events in New York on September 11, 2001, Boone drew over 100 clocks, each set to the time 9:11. Drawings of balls of fire and smoke from tall buildings with many windows were also created by Boone. Stillman suggests that autism demonstrates higher-vibrational capacities of senses consistent with the acute and often overwhelming sensations to sight, taste, touch and hearing.[65]

Not all experiments are conducted in laboratories. Drewes and Drucker in the 1970s conducted experiments in the homes of children using piles of M&M candies. Powell conducts telepathy experiments with children in their homes and British scientist Rupert Sheldrake has conducted experiments in schools with children. Sheldrake has studied telepathy and a sense of being stared at since the early 1980s, arguing for the non-locality of mind. Some of Sheldrake's recent research involves mothers and babies, and pets and their owners.[66] These studies show how mothers who are away from their babies can accurately record when their baby is anxious, hungry or distressed. This, according to Sheldrake, is more than the "let down" mechanism women experience when their baby is hungry (when their breasts fill with milk). In studies with animals, Sheldrake shows a staggering percentage of dogs and cats who know when their owners are arriving home. These behaviors point to telepathic communication that is developed between communities (including animals and humans).

A simple experiment was designed by Sheldrake and used to measure whether people know when others are staring at them. This experiment was trialed by teachers and students in five schools in the US and three schools in Germany. The experiment involved children working in pairs, one sitter and one looker. Lookers and sitters were separated by a 2-meter distance in a space that had no reflective objects such as mirrors or windows (to eradicate the possibility of the sitter seeing what the looker is doing). A score sheet was given to participants and the random trials began when the looker signaled, by using a clicker. The looker recorded on her/his sheet when he had looked at the sitter's head or if he/she has looked away and thought about something else. Statistical analysis showed an extremely significant case of positive scores (much higher than chance) from the school experiments, with children knowing when they are being stared at. My own research on the sense of being stared at in children was conducted through questionnaires, interviews and simple experiments with a group of different families. The results are consistent with Sheldrake's findings, with a significantly high percentage of children knowing when they are being stared at.

Children and Near-Death Experiences

The public was introduced to the concept of near-death experiences in the late 1960s through the work of Raymond Moody and his now classic book *Life After Life*. Other medical scientists such as Bruce Greyson, Kenneth Ring and Penny Sartori continue near-death studies, using mainly narrative enquiry combined with measurement scales. These studies are predominantly conducted on adults and measured using "the Greyson Scale". This is a measurement tool designed by Dr. Bruce Greyson, that uses the features of the classical model of an NDE (experiencing a tunnel, a light, other beings, acquiring wisdom and other realities) to compare near-death experiences with pathologies. The scale is based on the experiences of adults who have died for short periods of time. A research study I am currently co-leading with Pediatric specialist, Dr Graeme O'Connor,[67] explores near-death experiences with children aged between three and 12 years. At the time of writing, we are just starting fieldwork exploring with children unexplained experiences, defined medically as "delirium", following cardiac arrest and death for around 2-3 minutes. There is very little data to report here as the fieldwork has just begun but informal anecdotal evidence suggests children have unexplained experiences that share features of OBEs and NDEs. Graeme and I continue to identify experiences that carry features of "unexplained" experiences like the ones mentioned above.

Only a handful of researchers across the world are asking children to report what happened when they died. In the 1990s

Cherie Sutherland, an Australian researcher, published 18 cases of children's near-death experiences to support parents who had lost children, by spreading a blanket of comfort over those who are still grieving from one of life's most unbearable ruptures.[68] Sutherland collected the narratives of children, including several under the age of four years. The stories told by children and interviews conducted with parents show how children feel different to others following a near-death experience. The research also noted how children who have had an NDE are more likely to challenge mainstream religious doctrines and institutional contexts (such as education). Sutherland retells stories of children who met Jesus during their NDE experiences. These children take great umbrage with teachers, priests and other adults-in-authority, who try to tell them what Jesus looks like and what God is!

PMH Atwater is a leading author in children's near-death experiences and has researched the phenomena since the 1970s. Like Sutherland, Atwater notes how children can feel different from their family and peers following a near-death experience and question mainstream traditions and practices. In Atwater's book, *Children of the New Millennium: Children's Near-Death Experiences and the Evolution of Humankind,* correlations are made between children's NDEs and significant transformational changes in their intellect, sensitivities and attitudes. Atwater notes a sample of 277 children experiencers, with half of this number being young adults.

The methodology that Atwater uses is described as empirical and uses a mixture of questionnaires, interviews, observations and children's artwork. Atwater identifies four categories of NDE experience from her research: Initial Experience, Unpleasant Experience, Pleasant Experience and Transcendent Experience. For each of the categories Atwater compares statistical data for adults and children in her sample. Initial Experience is a loving nothingness or a living darkness with 76% of children and 20%

of adults experiencing this state. Unpleasant Experience is an encounter with a threatening world, akin to an inner cleansing experience, with children assigned a 3% incident rate and adults 15%. Pleasant Experience is defined as a heaven-like scenario with friends and family, with children showing a 19% incident rate and adults 47%. Transcendent Experiences are defined as exposure to otherworldly dimensions beyond the individual's frame of reference, with 2% of children experiencing this state and 18% of adults.[69]

If one was to approach the near-death experience as a subjective and conditioned one, these figures are unsurprising. If indeed unpleasant NDEs are self-cleansing processes (which research suggests is the case), we might expect adults to have more unpleasantness to clear than children. Furthermore, the low incidence of children meeting relatives in the "afterlife" could show a wisdom that adults may not yet possess – as the late Ram Dass reminds us, "if you think you're enlightened, go spend a week with your family"! Changes in children identified by Atwater include physiological and psychological, such as enhanced creativity, unusual sensitivity, electrical sensitivity and synesthesia – changes also reported by adult near-death experiencers. The data and insights offered by Atwater are incredibly valuable for developing approaches to supporting children who have had an NDE. Atwater highlights the important fact that children are often missing from near-death studies and her work addresses this deficit.

Before looking more closely at Atwater's approach to researching NDEs with children, it's important to recognize her dedication, longevity, and the contribution she has made to the field, as an NDE researcher. Atwater's methodology has come under fire from critics such as Harold Widdison, who wrote a review of Atwater's book in 2001.[70] Widdison's criticisms note inconsistency in statistics and sample numbers, noting that in total, 44 children participated in interviews and not 277, as is claimed by Atwater. Widdison highlights discrepancies with general claims about changes in children, especially as there is no data to evidence children's physiological and psychological traits before their NDE. Nor are there any references to brain imaging or scans to evidence any claims made about changes in the brain. To complicate matters further, several accounts are from adults who are reporting NDEs at birth or before the age of three years. Atwater's valuable insights and research claims are generated from the living experiences of children – including observations of their own "before and after NDE" states. Statistical data may be problematic in this type of research study as seen by Widdison's criticisms – this may show how good qualitative researchers feel they must appeal to the language of science (numbers, statistics etc.) to validate their own research findings. It also demonstrates that statistical data is not always necessary when exploring human experience.

My own observations of Atwater's methodology noted some ethical issues when researching with children. Atwater describes her role as a researcher to that of a "police officer" who interviews, observes and cross-checks information – while also using gestures and body language that police officers use to make witnesses talk. Atwater states that her role as a researcher is kept hidden from children, with the intention to keep conversations gentle. This shows Atwater to be a researcher attentive to children's well-being as she works around an incredibly sensitive topic with children. Yet this approach raises some ethical implications for researching with children. In research, children should provide *informed* consent that can only be given if children have all the information about the research they are involved in, how their data will be used, who the adult researcher is and why they are doing the research. Atwater does not allow parents to be present when interviewing children. In the research I conduct, children are offered choices about whether a parent, carer or supportive adult should be present. I am a stranger to children when I first meet them and some children (especially those who may have been hurt by an adult) prefer support. It is not often that adults are present in interviews; when they are, they stay near (not too near) and occupy themselves with other activities.

These criticisms are aimed at the methodology and not PMH Atwater, for whom I hold the greatest respect. Atwater has led the way for other researchers to explore NDEs with children, in a field that privileges numbers and experiments over narrative enquiry. It is challenging to involve children equitably in research practice. It is important that we get it right with children, not just for their well-being, but for the sake of qualitative research practice that is often undervalued in scientific research. Qualitative researchers are required to work harder to evidence or argue that narratives are a legitimate source of data, conveying experiential authority of living experience. The processes that sit behind researching with children are arduous, involving detailed ethical applications, methodological descriptions, other empirical evidence and being very clear about the researcher's position, biases and experiences. This is partly why studies can be difficult to start and take time to finish.

Children and Reincarnation

It is rare that subjective experiences of children can be evidenced, regardless of whether their experiences are mundane or extraordinary. Dr. Ian Stevenson did just this, documenting and evidencing over 2,500 cases of children's accounts of reincarnation. In 1957, Stevenson was appointed a Professor of Psychiatry and Chairman at the University of Virginia. Investigating the paranormal was not considered appropriate then (and this has not changed much in contemporary academia). In 1960, as luck would have it, or perhaps in a synchronistic way, Stevenson published an article on children and reincarnation, that was read by Chester F. Carlson, the founder of the Xerox machine. Excited by the article, Carlson began to fund and follow Stevenson's research. When Carlson died in 1968, he left a million dollars in his will to support Stevenson's research, enabling Stevenson to relinquish chairmanship duties and set up the Division of Perceptual Studies. When asked in an interview for *The New York Times* why he began his research into children and reincarnation, Stevenson replied: "discontent with other explanations of human personality. I wasn't satisfied with psychoanalysis or behaviorism or for that matter neuroscience. Something seemed to be missing."[71]

Towards the end of his life, Stevenson's research focused on the relationship between birthmarks of children who reported past lives and wound marks of the identified deceased individuals. Stevenson's book *European Cases of the Reincarnation Type* was published two years before his death in 2005. Stevenson highlights how little is known about why pigmented birthmarks occur in particular locations of the skin and notes how 35% of children who claim to remember past lives have birthmarks and/or birth defects that they attribute to wounds on a person whose life the child remembers.[72] Cases involving 210 children were recorded by Stevenson. In cases in which a deceased person was identified "the details of whose life unmistakably matched the child's statements; a close correspondence was nearly always found between the birthmarks and/or birth defects on the child and the wounds of the deceased person."[73] These astounding correlations raise questions about the relationship between mind and body – and the nature of matter itself. Over his thirty-plus years of researching children and reincarnation, Stevenson identified typical features of child reincarnation cases that are: talking about the life of an individual at a very young age (this can be family members or strangers); recognition of places the child has never visited; same phobias related to how the deceased individual died; and play that mimics the previous occupation of the deceased.

Dr. Jim Tucker assisted Stevenson with his research and continues to study children and reincarnation today, using multiple methods and maintaining the rigorous approaches of Dr. Stevenson. Tucker is a child psychiatrist and Professor of Psychiatry at the University of Virginia and has written several books on the subject. Tucker follows up cases that have been reported by interviewing children with family members present. This is the start of the research process. At times, Tucker reports using controlled tests to see if children recognize friends of the deceased individual whose memories the child recalls.[74] Tucker developed a scale measure to assess the relative strength of children's claims to remember previous lives. The scale is designed to assign weight to features of each case "that are more suggestive of a paranormal experience."[75] A total of 799 cases were analyzed with the measurement scale, showing a high degree of consistency. Some results indicated that the strength of a case correlated with a child's economic status but not his or her social caste or status. The strength of cases did not correlate with initial attitudes of parents – but did with early sets of statements about previous lives, made by the child. The scale recognized high correlations of strength of cases with intense emotions of the child and facial resemblance of the child with the deceased person.

A famous case that Tucker explored was that of a young boy named James Leininger, published in *Explore* journal in 2016. James Leininger is from Louisiana in the US. From the age of two years, James made statements and demonstrated behaviors that implied he remembered the life of an American pilot killed during World War II. The case had a significant public profile with James' parents engaging in television programs and writing a book about their experiences. Tucker used the information already collated by James' father to carry out a detailed investigation of the evidence.

Tucker notes how James gave his parents specific and detailed information about being in a plane that was shot down by the Japanese. James was only 28 months old when these details were reported. The information James relayed was the name of the pilot, the boat he was stationed on and the place where his plane was shot down. When James was old enough to draw, he created pictures depicting battle scenes involving planes. Tucker reports that James signed his pictures "James 3". When James' parents questioned him about the number three, James explained that he was the third James. The name of the pilot that James reported memories of was James Huston, or James Jr. – making James the third. What is remarkable about James' case is that another soldier, Jack Larsen, who served with James Huston had survived the war. James' father met with Jack and learned that only one pilot from the ship (named by baby James) had been lost during the battle, a 21-year-old named James M. Huston, Jr.

I have come across reports of past life memories in my own research with children demonstrating many of the features Tucker notes, such as play mimicking the role of the deceased person or personality, nightmares, intense phobias, extreme emotions and familiarity with places they have never visited before. As I do not research children's past life memories exclusively or aim to evidence them, I do not attempt to follow up their claims. It is interesting, however, that the features identified by Stevenson and Tucker can be seen in children who report past life memories. Tucker acknowledges different criticisms about the case of James Leininger, with accusations of the reports being fantasy, trauma from visiting the airfield or fraud enacted by the parents. It becomes clear through Tucker's well thought out reprisals that none of these are the case. Theories of James' demonstrating psi abilities by accessing thoughts through a "thought pool" have been proposed by other academics.[76] Tucker suggests that thought pools cannot account for children's reports of intermission periods between lives. My own view is that this argument cannot discount the idea that children can access "thought pools". Other types of children's experiences, such as telepathy and senses of being stared at, suggest that children are already accessing thoughts. Whether thoughts belong to pools or fields is something I explore more in later chapters.

Moving Forward

The examples included in this chapter show how distinguished scientists and researchers provide evidence of children who can read minds, continue to have conscious experiences after bodily death, remember previous lives and know when someone is staring at them. These scientists have devoted long periods of time and resources to their studies with children. Mainstream science, academia and health institutions are still resistant to use evidence from these studies to inform policy and practice. Researchers who decide to investigate unexplained experiences in children (and adults) struggle to find institutional support and funding for studies. There is a growing body of academics researching adults' unexplained experiences with more universities offering courses and PhD scholarships in these areas. As a lecturer in a university, I supervise postgraduate and PhD students. I have yet only met one PhD student who is studying unexplained experiences in childhood. It is time to bring the work together, to form a strong alliance, to share different approaches and disciplinary knowledge and to learn from each other.

Studies often focus on one type of experience with children. This is valuable as it affords deeper exploration into different facets of the experience. For example, deep studies of children's reincarnation stories involve cross-checking information with public records and other documentation. This is not possible with all unexplained experiences. This is where experiments can prove very useful for validating experiences such as telepathy and other forms of non-local communication. Exploring the presence of a range of unexplained experiences in childhood can provide a picture of how common these types of experiences are. Importantly, a fuller understanding of unexplained experiences in childhood can inform how we understand the nature of self, mind and reality. When children are afforded spaces to co-interpret and reflect on their own living experiences, this can enrich knowledge generated from studies. The motivation for researching unexplained experiences with children is important. For example, are we researching near-death experiences to find out, "What happens when we die?" This is the wrong question. A better question to ask is, "Who/what are we?" When this question is explored, all other questions become redundant. If we try to explain the "unexplained" from the conventional scientific position, we are trying to understand how a separate biological entity can read another's mind or leave their body, go to heaven and come back. Even the language we use can betray the starting point.

Children's agency in experimental research needs to be strongly considered. Traditional scientific methodology in lab-based and experimental studies often position participants as objects and their experiences measured. Value is placed on objectivity while subjectivity is viewed as mere anecdote, lacking scientific validity. Peter Fenwick, a scientist and researcher of near-death experiences, suggests that science cannot refute nor confirm subjective accounts of experience. As Kuhn asks, can any scientific experiment ever be truly objective?[77] There is an underlying assumption in traditional research practice that there are objective truths that can be measured. For example, involving children in neuroscientific research advances knowledge concerning cause and effect, but can close down opportunities to consider the diversity and immeasurability of human experience. The insightful meanings children assign to their unexplained experiences are not given space in studies of this kind. What may be needed is more qualitative and participatory approaches with children and a critical approach towards the agendas and worldviews that as researchers we start from. It's about having the courage to do research differently. In the next chapter I discuss some of my own studies.

Chapter 5

A Return to Unexplained Experiences *with* Children

I believe there is much more to life than our brains... to be able to feel what someone else is feeling or sense things that you couldn't have possibly known... shows we are much more in tune with our self and others than we consciously know.

Kassie, aged 17 years

How adults and wider society respond to children's unexplained experiences has implications for children's well-being – and for the future of our next generation. The studies that have been included so far have been experimental, relying on chi-squares, statistical measures and other research tools associated with physicalist models of research activity. These ways of researching unexplained experience are vitally important for understanding any fundamental mechanisms that underlie psi experience and its potential impact on matter. Research that considers influences such as psychological, physiological, environmental and cultural aspects is equally important when trying to understand the mystery of human experience. One step further takes us to an approach called *participatory research*, where subjective living experience is the primary data and a source of expert authority. I discuss the important role of participatory research in this chapter for exploring unexplained experiences with children. I also include children's experiences collected from several of my own research studies and discuss the language of unexplained experience in children.

Participatory Research in a Participatory Universe

For the past 18 years, I have had the pleasure to research with children of all ages and backgrounds. From babies to teenagers, children with disabilities, homeless young people, trauma-experienced children, young people from ethnic minority communities, care-experienced children and so on. I have worked with large organizations such as Save the Children, exploring with children issues such as neglect and abuse; and the Council of Europe, examining inequality with young people who are discriminated against. For 10 years, I was employed as a Research Manager for local government, developing ways to involve citizens (including adults) in policy-making research, intended to positively affect their lives. I finished my PhD and decided to remain in the community with boots-on-the-ground, rather than pursue a career in academia. I believed that researching with people would empower them, by ensuring their voices would be heard in processes of service development and policy making.

Researching with people to inform change meant developing ways for doing research that would ensure people become active agents rather than passive objects. Historically, qualitative research has excluded persons-without-voice, due to its specialized languages (numbers, statistics, scientific discourses) and the valuing of certain types of knowledges. Participatory research challenges traditional ways of doing research, that often exclude the living experiences of everyday people. It is an approach that positions people at the heart of research practice, valuing their knowledge and living experiences as valuable research data – through critical praxis (informing theory from practice). Participatory research is under-utilized in health and scientific research although a growing interest in the value of people's living experiences is happening across disciplines such as the health sciences. Unexplained experiences are subjective experiences that are not often shared in "real-time" with others, with some exceptions such as shared death experiences, or groups of people witnessing apparitions or UFOs. Much like our intimate experiences such as thoughts and feelings, they are difficult to "evidence" in empirical ways. Empiricism advocates evidence based on shared experiences through the physical senses. In this way many experiences, like the unexplained ones described above, are not taken seriously. In qualitative research, an experience is taken seriously if it is largely reported by many people. Unexplained experiences are reported in this way but still never considered serious enough to change policy and evoke social transformation.

A convergence of my research interests with my own experiences, outlined at the start of the book (and others that continued into adulthood), led me to do the work I do today with children. Over the years, researching in the field of social science has led me to conclude that:

1. The stories that people tell in research are synonymized with their "self" or who they are – this can create and sustain a limited experience of self, human suffering and separation from others and the natural world.

2. People are mainly viewed as individual fixed beings that are separate from others and the world.

3. People's senses of self are shaped through the language practices (discourses) of social institutions and systems – social systems construct and sustain individualism and competition between people.

4. There is no consensus on what we are as human beings; self and subjective experience continues to be a mystery.

5. Social systems and institutions are rooted in a physicalist metaphysics (stating that our subjective experiences of self, others and the world emerge from material things – such as brains).

6. Children and adults commonly have experiences that challenge conventional ideas of personhood, time and space; children and adults cannot/do not wish to share

these experiences due to social stigma or fear of being diagnosed/categorized as mentally ill.

7. Only certain types of experiences are included in social research with people; experiences that challenge conventional ideas of personhood, time and space are normally excluded from social research.

When people are invited into research so scientists, scholars and researchers can access experiential knowledge (what we know from our own experiences), we start from unexplored claims about the experiencer – the one who experiences. Research agendas start from scientists themselves or organizations that are funding the research. In this way, only certain types of experiences will be asked for and listened to. This leads to all kinds of questions about the "authority" of the one who is reporting living experience, regardless of how "participatory" a study is. The studies I do with children are attempting to address this oversight. Instead of starting from adult and/or organizational agendas, research begins from children's agendas and by exploring the experiencer – the nature of the one who is reporting experiences.

Exploring unexplained experiences enhances self-enquiry, as they are experiences that push people beyond the boundaries of their own stories, or personhood. Children who have unexplained experiences can already sense a self which extends beyond the boundaries of their ages, forms, desires, fears and aspirations (see chapter 6 for fuller discussion of self and children's unexplained experiences). As mentioned earlier, younger children may see unexplained experiences as the norm. Older children have developed layers of belief, and this can be seen when we analyze their personal narratives of self. Words and references (discourse) from mental health, education and other adults, pervade their personal stories. Once children closely examine this, either through sharing and reflecting on their unexplained experiences or through self-enquiry research activities, they can become the author of their stories, critically conscious of their sense of self and how it can affect their experience of the world.[78]

Participatory research is about relations between people, processes and the world. It emphasizes co-creation, seeing people and researchers as mutable, active co-creators within an interactive field of being and becoming. Relationality is a popular model in social research, with people referred to as social actors who can co-create change, through their own knowledge and experiences. In good conditions, when policymakers are involved, and resources are available, participatory research can be a powerful conduit for co-creating social transformation. This model has been extended/or has been informed by the idea that the universe is "participatory", created by observers through a "participatory anthropic principle", a term coined by the physicist John Wheeler. Wheeler suggested that people co-create with the universe as "participants in bringing into being not only the near and here, but the far away and long ago."[79]

A connected movement between people and an evolving universe is proposed by Wheeler. Relations between things is a useful way to conceive of how co-creation of realities can occur. Providing that relationality is not taken to be all that there *is*. Thinking about relations shows the complexity of human beings, the world and the universe as they evolve – but doesn't really address what things *are*. Fundamental reality may not be so complex (I return to this idea in later chapters). The point here is to highlight the participatory nature of human beings, animals and nature, in co-creating our experiences and realities. In this way, models of research that do not account for relations and the participatory nature of our shared reality, captures only parts of the whole. Participatory research approaches are used with children who take part in studies. In this way, their living experiences and the meanings assigned to them by children are considered as valuable data.

Image 3: A Strange Experience, Aged 14 years

Some Current Studies

The program of research I'm involved in aims to explore the nature of "self" and unexplained experiences, through a living-experience lens. There are many studies that explore experiences with children, but you will not find many that include the *unexplained* or explore the nature of self. There are several studies that are part of this program, some are finished while others are ongoing, or just beginning. It can take several months just to start up a small pilot study with children because of ethics applications, involving children in design and searching for funding to do the research. Studies with children use different methods such as art, play, storytelling, sound (music-making, sounds etc.), drama and photography/filmmaking. Studies also include more traditional research methods such as interviews and questionnaires. Sometimes, children can take on a lead role in the research. For example, in our current near-death study, we have a group of young researchers with experience of being in hospital. Their role is to co-design research methods that can be used with very sick or non-verbal children. So far, the young researchers have designed a play research method for very young children who have experienced cardiac arrest. This involves using small world toys (toy figures of hospital rooms and equipment), so children can "play-out" what they may have experienced during and after their cardiac arrest. Analysis of data can involve working with linguistic and semiotic analytical frameworks (analyzing features of language and images and their relationships to other social domains) and statistical data. Visual data is often interpreted through the lens of children's reflections, depth psychology, metaphorical analysis and studies from archaeology. I was once criticized as "trying to untangle spaghetti", a comment made about the research I am involved in. These are criticisms often made by scholars who work in tightly framed disciplinary boxes. Understanding the mystery of being human and unexplained experiences requires an interdisciplinary and collaborative approach, more like weaving a tapestry, than untangling spaghetti.

Table 2 shows unexplained experiences of children identified through a small study in 2019, that demonstrate the kinds of experiences often reported by children:

Table 2: Examples of Unexplained Experiences of Children

Type	%	Count
Seeing beings or animals that other people can't see	33	6
Have been in serious accident or in hospital and had visions or other experiences	11	2
Had an out of body experience (where you feel you have left your body)	27	5
Had sleep paralysis (where you feel awake but you cannot move your body)	27	5
Felt one with the universe or the world	11	2
Know what other people are thinking	11	2
Know what other people are feeling	16	3
Had unusual or lucid dreams	61	11
Heard sounds, singing or voices that other people can/cannot hear	16	3
Other	5	1
		16ps

The table and percentages are based on a very small sample of children and young people. What the table shows is a range of unexplained experiences that children report. Some of these experiences, such as visions and voice-hearing, can be quickly labelled as disorders by well-meaning adults. Other experiences, such as lucid or exceptional dreams, seem to be more socially accepted. Here are a couple of example studies that capture process and some findings:

"Being Connected"

The "Being Connected" study is showing how children participate in the world in a very intra-connected way. Children report experiences that suggest minds may be non-local and affect matter in ways that we don't yet understand. The "Being Connected" study began at the start of 2020 to explore in more detail how children experience connections between self, others and the world in unexplained ways. There are three parts to this research: simple experiments with children and families, online questionnaires, and interviews with children and young people. Interviews with children (as part of this study) are showing how children are very conscious of subtle connections that exist between self, others and the world. Children often report strong unseen connections with animals, such as the case of Carly who described a telepathic connection between herself and her dog. Carly described how her dog will know when she is in trouble or feeling sad when Carly is not physically near Bobby (the dog). Bobby will seek out Carly, find her and support or comfort her. Children seem to have a strong connection with their animal friends.

So far, interviews with children have identified telepathic connections between siblings, knowing when someone is being stared at, premonitions about everyday events and experiencing others' feelings and bodily sensations. One child described how he can make objects fall off walls, just by focusing his attention on them. The questionnaire data is showing similar results. A very high percentage of children report a sense of being stared at, to turn around and see that someone is staring at them. Some children state that they have this experience while alone, feeling that someone is staring at them, only this cannot be verified (with a starer), as the starer is not visible to the physical eye. When I ask children if this feels the same to when they are outside and sense someone staring at them, the response is "yes", showing children's sense of being stared at while alone carries the same experiential features of while not alone. The next phase of this research is to set up simple experiments in homes and other places, to examine some of the experiences children are reporting. Some of these experiments are modelled on Rupert Sheldrake's *simple experiments* (see chapter 3).

Included here are quotes from children who have taken part in the "Being Connected" study:

I often feel other people's emotions, especially negative feelings (aged 17 years)
I feel connected to trees and nature for some reason (aged 14 years)
I know when things are going to happen (aged 8 years)
I get a weird feeling in my back before someone actually touches it (aged 14 years)
I stared at the picture and it fell off the wall and then it happened again (aged 9 years)

Children shared how these experiences made them feel:

They can feel weird but it feels like a superpower sometimes (aged 14 years)
I can't remember all my experiences... they make me feel spiritual when I'm aware of them (aged 15 years)
It means connection (aged 12 years)

Children appear to be very aware of subtle connections we share between others and the world. For younger children who took part in the study, being connected to others and the world seems almost natural to them. That is why it is very difficult to explore "Being Connected" with younger children. It seems to be a natural way of being in the world for very young children.

Our "Unusual" Experiences

Some of the research I have conducted around unexplained experiences in general (frequency in children, types of experiences, narrative accounts etc.) has been done as an independent researcher/observer. This is different from my academic role, in that experiences are reported in more natural settings and contexts by children. In all my roles (researcher, volunteer, parent, friend), I hear children report unexplained experiences. Now, I don't meet a child and start to ask them strange questions about their experiences! How children report their experiences can happen in a variety of ways. For example, adults who know about the type of work I do will contact me about their children's unexplained experiences. Mostly I will talk with their child about their experiences, sometimes I won't. This depends on whether the child is happy for their parent or carer to share their experiences. In other cases, I can be involved in voluntary work (supporting in schools, supporting young people's well-being) and will hear about children's experiences when they share their stories. If it's appropriate, we will discuss them in detail. It is not always possible and depends on how they make sense of them or want to discuss them. As a parent, I am in contact with lots of other parents, at a football club for example and other places where there are lots of children. I hear so many incidences of unexplained experiences – perhaps this is because I have "an ear for them" due to the work that I do. In my professional research, I actively seek to engage with children who report unexplained experiences. Their experiences are collated, analyzed and distributed through strict ethical and research protocols.

Experiences that are shared with me, when I support young people in crisis, can be remarkable – in how they share the qualities of experiences referred to as psi or paranormal. Some of these children have already been in the system, diagnosed with one disorder or another. Hidden within their distressing experiences are other experiences that bring them hope and excitement. Sometimes they equip children with a fresh way to consider who they may be in the difficult world around them. Although I have researched with hundreds of children across the years, catching instances of unexplained experiences, there are not yet large numbers of children represented in these studies. This is partly because participatory-qualitative research does not aim to accumulate statistical information about how many children, for example, experience telepathy. Instead, smaller numbers of children allow for deeper exploratory practices that are needed to understand senses of self and living experiences. However, it is also important in research to try to show the prevalence, durability and statistical measure of a phenomenon, and children's experiences are now recorded in a database that will start to show the "ordinariness" of experiences viewed as non-ordinary.

Here are some examples of experiences from the database:

Telepathy

Billy was out with his friend. They reached the bottom of the street and Billy *thought*, "Something doesn't seem right here." His friend turned to Billy and *replied*, "Yeah, I think you're right about that, mate."

Near-Death Experience

Hamid was in intensive care and very ill. His mother reported how Hamid began to describe moving towards a door, another place, as his vitals became worse. He told his mother that he wasn't ready to leave her. At this point, Hamid began to recover.

Apparitions

Poppy had recently moved into an old home with her family. Poppy reported nightly visits from a being who shapeshifted into different beings (animals and people that she knew). This happened consistently over a few nights.

Engaging with Beings

Chris described meetings with beings that he viewed as "aliens" or not of this world. These meetings were reported in hypnogogic states (between sleep and waking). Chris noted a realness that affected him in waking hours.

Some of the academic research I do focuses on unexplained experiences of children in different cultural contexts, gathering children's experiences through online questionnaires. This will eventually lead to fieldwork with children in the countries who are supporting the study (India, Brazil, US, Switzerland, France, UK and others). The data collected through earlier studies show a range of unexplained experiences had by a diverse set of children (i.e. some had medical conditions, some did not etc.). The questionnaire is gathering similar experiences of children across a global context, allowing for influences such as culture, religiosity, geographical location and other factors to be taken into consideration. For example, Mateus Donia Martinez, a scholar who is supporting the research, is studying mediumship in children in Brazil. In some sections of Brazilian culture, mediumship is a taken for granted experience, tied strongly to cultural and religious beliefs. The study is starting to show how children's unexplained experiences are understood in very different ways across diverse cultural contexts – and how this can affect a child's being and becoming in the world.

The Language of Children's Unexplained Experiences

In the 2002 movie *Dragonfly*, Kevin Costner plays a doctor who is contacted by his deceased wife through his patients who have had NDEs. In the movie, Costner's character follows a symbolic trail to a children's hospice, where young patients are drawing strange images, that turn out to be clues, leading the doctor to a remote island. On the island, he finds his baby daughter, left there when his wife's body was washed up onto the shore. The doctor's deceased wife had a birthmark in the shape of a dragonfly and the movie focuses on this symbol, as representing hope and self-transformation. Costa & Soares, in their 2014 article "Free as a butterfly: symbology and palliative care", discuss the intriguing presence of butterflies on the walls and windows of hospitals. The authors conclude that the butterfly symbolizes metamorphosis, with death perceived as a possibility for renewal – the breaking of the cocoon is the death of the body, when the soul achieves freedom in the image of the butterfly. Signs and symbols are a language of the unconscious, often used when our experiences cannot be explained through conventional language systems. Sometimes children cannot represent their unexplained experiences through language. This is not merely a result of their own linguistic capabilities; rather it is because language does not have the capacity to represent a full spectrum of human experiences. We see this when adults who have an NDE return and try to report all the nuances of their experience. They can't find a word to represent a color, or what they were feeling. Many of the studies I do with children will involve using art or mark making that can support how they represent their unexplained experiences.

We mostly read and navigate the world through images. For those of us that drive cars, we may not realize that we engage in semiosis, reading symbols such as traffic lights, to ensure we reach our destination safely. As traffic lights turn red, we know that the light is signaling to stop. The traffic light does not use words yet still we know its meaning and heed its command (if we are responsible drivers!). Red traffic lights that signal "stop" are used across the world; we read the light in the same way regardless of our language differences. The sign is universal. We may not notice how much we engage with the world through symbols and pictographs. Think about the symbols on washing machines or on the side of packaging. Roland Barthes, a French sociologist and "father of semiosis" (images as language), recognized the role of symbols as a system of signs that we read. Some signs carry universal meanings while others are more culturally specific; either way human beings are very apt at making meanings from sign and symbol. Many ancient societies used pictorial symbols as their writing systems, for examples the hieroglyphics used by the ancient Egyptians, or the ancient script of Uruk (Iraq), thought to be the first formal writing system. These and others are complex systems and very little is known about how they emerged. Some of the oldest known symbols are thought to be between 70,000-500,000 years old, zigzag patterns etched into everyday artefacts such as shells, clay and sand. Images, symbols and patterns seem to be a language of unexplained experiences, used by children to convey some of their experiences.

Genevieve Von Petzinger is the granddaughter of a World War II codebreaker and a brave archaeologist who explores caves to find simple symbols etched by ancient people. In her book, *The First Signs: Unlocking the Mysteries of the World's Oldest Symbols*, Von Petzinger suggests that simple symbols, such as triangles, circles and squiggles, could represent the start of the first human code. Von Petzinger identified symbols found in caves across Europe. Across a 30,000 year time span, Von Petzinger identified only 32 exact signs, repeating across space and time. With sixty-five percent of these symbols staying across time. These same signs or consistent doodles were also found outside Europe. The signs carry a universality that seems to transcend culture, time and physical space and no one seems to know why. Some scholars claim that these types of marks are symbolic of shared human experiences, while others offer a reductionist view, linking the geometrical shapes to early visual cortex functions (how the eyes work). The entoptic explanation suggests that visual patterns are hardwired into our vision. This explanation of biological hardwiring may not fit with biological evolution theories – if humans evolve biologically, these patterns will change over time.

These spiral images were drawn by a little girl aged five who has frequent unexplained experiences (such as seeing beings and exceptional dreams).

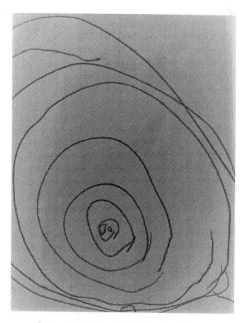

Image 4: A portal to Another Place

Lexy began to draw a series of spirals. I asked Lexy, "What is this you're drawing?" Lexy replied very casually, "It's a portal to another place." The word "portal" is not often used by children as young as Lexy. So, I asked, "Where did you get this word from?" She shrugged her shoulders and proceeded to explain how portals can move you from one world into another. Younger children tend to draw in scribbles, mark making is seen as a prerequisite to more refined forms of art and writing. How younger children draw is often described through social explanations. Linguist, Gunther Kress, argues how children act multi-modally "in the things they use, the objects they make, and in the engagement of their bodies there is no separation of body and mind."[80] The natural and flexible actions of mark making in younger children shows an unselfconsciousness that adult artists only dream of attaining.[81] Marks demonstrate an interplay between inner and outer worlds for children. Images like the ones above contain symbols viewed as universal such as spirals, circles and squiggles. Symbols as the essence of being human, their creation liberating children from space and time. Patterns and other symbolic representations were created by older children to represent a sense of self when experiencing unexplained phenomena (see below "Unexplained Experiences and Universal Symbols"). Symbology was also identified in artwork produced by older children:

Image 5: "I" of the Soul

Image 6: Talking with Grandmother

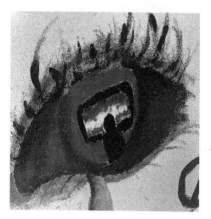

Image 7: Illusion of the World

The children and young person who created these images could not explain linguistically some of their unexplained experiences. Both Images 5 and 7 show how the symbol of the human eye was often used to represent a deeper aspect of self, one that experiences unexplained phenomena. In Image 5 (aged 8 years) the child has drawn a field of energy around the head of the figure, which is representing the *"space suit"* of the child. The large eye in the center of the head connotes the "I" of the child but also the "I" of the whole universe. In Image 7, the self-portrait of the young person is centered in the large eye, looking out onto multiple layers of reality. The screen denotes how this child considers the world to be an illusion, due to her unexplained experiences and expanded perceptions of self and reality. The color red represents her own struggles in the social world. Image 6 shows one way in which this young person communicates with her deceased grandmother. This image represents her communications in hypnogogic states where her grandmother provides information through memory images, that she passes on to her family. In this scene, the grandmother shares a memory from her youth, a happy scene that took place long ago. To the left of the picture is the young person situated behind a *window*. This was described as a translucent barrier between herself and her grandmother. The use of symbol can be seen with the human eye, musical symbols (denoting happiness) and color. Metaphorical representations are used in the images, such as the television screen in Image 6 and the physical eye used to represent the *I* of experience.

Unexplained Experiences and Universal Symbols

Psychologist and psychedelic researcher, Dr. David Luke, notes how there are few scholars that attempt to address the assumptions about geometrical shapes from an experiential position. Luke advances a neuropsychological model of entoptic phenomena, proposing that the non-figurative images are in fact universal representations, once perceived by our shamanic ancestors during altered states of consciousness.[82] Carl Jung identified the mandala as a visual representation of the archetypal "Self", through research with patients, direct experience and studies of different cultures, religiosity and myth. The prevalence of geometrical shapes in nature is studied through fractal geometry. Fractals are fragmented geometric shapes that can be spilt into parts, which are smaller versions of the whole and can be found throughout nature. Etzel Cardeña makes connections between self-representation, art and anomalous experiences. Cardeña notes how art can represent subjective, anomalous experiences in objective ways through patterns found in nature, representing an underlying reality prior to space and time. It seems symbols that transcend culture, time and space may represent shared and collect experience for humans. Children and young people can default to patterns to represent their sense of self, when there are no words or concrete descriptions that can convey who they are. Below is a visual representation by a young male aged 17 years old that represents "who he is" during a peak or mystical experience in nature.

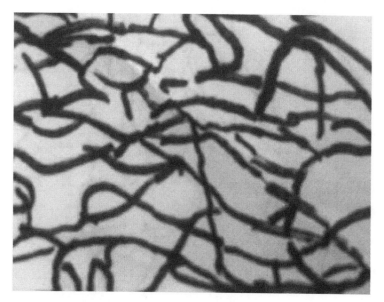

Image 8: "This is Me"

The pattern represents how this young person became connected to the environment when his sense of self expanded out to the universe. This visual representation of self is very similar to how people from pre-literate ancient cultures made marks in different materials such as wood and cave walls. Societies and cultures change through the ebb and flow of evolution, yet some aspects of being human (and how we express them) may remain consistent and untouched by time.

Advancing Research into Children's Unexplained Experiences

The last three chapters have highlighted the different ways for thinking about unexplained experiences of children, either as mental disorders, psychic abilities, expanded human cognition or everyday experiences. Explanations are located in different scholarship and ways of theorizing human beings, the world and its underlying reality. They are seeking tangible explanations about children's unexplained experiences within limited frameworks of materialism. This includes my own studies that can be highly governed by institutional rules and conditioned by my own understandings as a researcher. There has been little advancement in studying children's unexplained experiences across time. The common thread running through research, past and present, is how unexplained experiences are an extension of our natural human cognitive and perceptual experiences. This points to a need to understand who we are in our naturalness. What does it mean to be human and how does this correspond with our realities? Questions about "ontology" or what *is* are often substituted by questions that appeal to correlations between things, for example, "Did that mind act on that object?" We still seem to be working from assumptions about what things are and how they may be related to each other. Yet things such as mind or matter, or minds and minds, may not be as separate as they appear. It is now important to attend to the deeper and more difficult questions about the nature of self, mind, matter and reality, in the pursuit of trying to understand unexplained experiences of children. The rest of the book will venture through this dialogue, exploring unexplained experiences in relation to self, consciousness and reality.

Chapter 6

Unexplained Experiences of Children and the Nature of Self

Very young children still have an awareness of mythological contents, and if these contents remain conscious too long, the individual is threatened by an incapacity for adaptation... haunted by a constant yearning to remain with or to return to the original vision. There are very beautiful descriptions of these experiences by mystics and poets.
Jung (1935/1977, p. 95)

I believe that any state you're in can be overturned by looking inside yourself... this is why the sky and clouds idea for who we are is important.
Val, aged 13 years

When a child has an experience that goes beyond usual ideas of time and space, their sense of personhood can be disrupted. This tends to happen more with some types of unexplained experiences than others. For example, when children and young people have peak or mystical experiences, their sense of self expands. Their individual sense of identity is dissolved and replaced by a knowing of being, involving feeling one with the universe. Other types of unexplained experiences such as out of body experiences, having visions or hearing sounds, mirror Jung's descriptions of children's awareness of mythological and collective experiences. If experiences are fleeting, the usual self quickly integrates and anchors again into the world. If a child frequently has these types of experiences, integration and grounding becomes difficult.

Babies present other interesting ways to consider who we

are. For a while, babies do not differentiate between their own bodies and their mother's breast. Infants and younger children reside in what Lacan refers to as *the register of the real*, an unconditioned aperspectival consciousness[83] (prior to all perspectives). Suzanne Zeedyk suggests babies make meaning through patterns, constructing meaning-stories in different ways. As adults, our own "baby stories" are still available albeit unconscious to us. It seems, a sense of self, an *experiencer*, may be present before language emerges and the ego develops. As the poet Wordsworth reminds us:

> Our birth is but a sleep and a forgetting.
> The soul that rises
> With us, our life's star...
> Not in entire forgetfulness
> And not in utter nakedness
> But trailing clouds of glory do we come
> (1815)

This chapter examines the relationship between children's unexplained experiences and the nature of self. Looking at that simple but profound question "who am 'I'?" Jung (in the opening quote) refers to children having to let go of their sense of the original vision to adapt. Yet, the reality that children are being required to adapt into has become so far removed from their natural sense of self, that integration is becoming less possible. The rise of behaviors in children labelled as oppositional or ADHD may attest to a children's revolt against a reality that just isn't making sense. In this chapter, I examine theories about child development and the self – and how this relates to children's unexplained experiences. In the west, there are fixed ways for thinking about how children develop through stages, having implications for how children and their experiences are measured.

Developing Children and Self

Before the 18ᵗʰ century enlightenment era, children were viewed as inherently evil and products of original sin. This idea about children came from religious doctrines, informed by Platonian ideas about pre-existing forms that influence our behaviors in the world. Children were viewed as morally corrupt and polluted. French philosopher, Jean-Jacques Rousseau's (1712-1778) "nature child" suggested children to be inherently good, innocent and close to nature. Rousseau noted that children were feared and expelled by adults, who were reminded of their natural impulses in a time that required harsh social etiquettes. Rousseau's views contradicted the Catholic mainstream views of the time and copies of Rousseau's books were burned on the streets of Paris.[84] When Sigmund Freud announced that children were "tabula rasa" (blank slates) in the 19ᵗʰ century, parents became accountable for their children's moral behavior.

Jean Piaget, a famous child psychologist, published his first scientific paper aged 11. Piaget has influenced how children are understood in the modern world, with many disciplines such as education, child psychology and language acquisition, using the Piaget child development model. Piaget was interested in how children acquire knowledge and proposed a set of categories to measure when children would develop certain cognitive capacities. For example, children aged between birth and two years entered the sensorimotor stage, knowing the world through movements and sensations. In this stage, children have a sense of object permanence, and as they move towards the end of this stage, a sense they are separate to others. The preoperational stage (children aged 2-7 years) is where children learn to develop symbolic thought, become egocentric and think about things in concrete terms. The concrete operational stage (aged 7-11 years) proposed by Piaget states that children start to understand that their thoughts are unique to them and not necessarily shared by others. It marks a movement away from a shared sense of being towards an individual ego structure.

Albert Einstein called Piaget's model "so simple only a genius could have thought of it."[85] Yet there has been much criticism of how Piaget's model is understood and applied. In mainstream practice, children's selves and experiences tend to be measured according to different stages of Piaget's model. If children of a certain age do not meet the stages proposed by the model, they are often seen as under developing or not meeting the mark. In the early 1960s, the meaning of the word autism was used to describe schizophrenic states in adults. The word *autism* experienced a radical shift, when epidemiological and statistical studies were growing. Autism as a term was used as a category to describe hallucinations and unconscious fantasy life in infants, theorized through the work of Piaget and others.[86] It is an example of how models such as Piaget's can offset new types of "disorders", that view children as fixed entities, rather than dynamic beings.

Developing intelligence, or rather a certain kind of intelligence (rational thinking, hypothesizing and conceptual thinking) is what, according to Piaget, distinguishes adults from children. In Piaget's model, the child is progressing towards a formal operational stage that is found in children over 12 and adults. The term itself presupposes this stage is optimum for engaging or *operationalizing* in the world. Therefore, children are measured in terms of becoming-adult, as some ultimate level to be reached. The model implicitly presumes children's cognitive experiences and behaviors are inherent to the individual child. With logic and conceptual thinking being highly valued in the western world, other types of intelligences (such as feeling the world) become devalued. One only has to think about the incredible speed in which infants develop a wide range of cognitive and motor skills in the first two years of life, to recognize the problems with narrow ideas of intelligence. Despite mainstream adoption of Piaget's model, a growing body of scholarship is highly critical of its implications for children.

Since the early 1990s, childhood theorists such as David Oswell have challenged traditional constructions of children and child development theories which fix and objectify children.[87]

Another child prodigy, philosopher Ken Wilber, draws on Piaget's child development theories to develop a model of consciousness. In Wilber's earlier work (circa 1980s), a baby exists in an *unconscious* state, in a primary relationship to her mother (the mother archetype). The infant has no sense of a separate identity and is in a *chthonic* (underworld, netherworld) state of oneness with the collective unconscious. This undifferentiated matrix is followed by the sensori-physical stage, where the young child begins to develop an identity through sensing the external world, engaging physically or in a concrete way. Wilber proposes other developmental stages that are pre-personal or before the ego. There is magical thinking where the child uses different schemas (cognitive frameworks) to make sense of the world, and a stage where children start to internalize the social roles and rules of the world around him (this mirrors Piaget's concrete-operational stage). Wilber adds to Piaget's developmental model through additional stages that move from pre-personal, personal to transpersonal. For example, Wilber's Centaur stage sees the "self" start to transcend the ego-mind and integrate all stages gone before – including the Jungian shadow aspects of our unconscious inner life. Maslow refers to this as *self-actualization* – when a human being achieves a level of autonomy and integration. The next stages move beyond the personal (transpersonal) and can trigger unexplained or psychic experiences. Wilber suggests at this stage, people can transcend aspects of the individual such as gender identity. The stages carry on until self reaches a non-dual state. This experience of self is where the world arises in one's own being, with the sense that self or being is prior and beyond anything that arises within it.

Children as Natural Mystics?

Wilber's earlier writings suggest a pre/trans fallacy. The fallacy, according to Wilber, is that children have a heightened spiritual sensibility or can experience oneness in the same way as the adult mystics. Wilber instead views infants as in a state of alienation "from all the higher worlds whose total integration constitutes mysticism."[88] In this way, infants must evolve into a higher state, achieving a union with God or oneness. Wilber describes the pre-egoic state of infants as a mystical regression, alluding to troublesome influences from mainstream childhood development theories. Therefore, children cannot have access to transpersonal realms because their egos are not fully formed, as union must first pass through a separation (the development of the ego). As discussed in the last chapter, in my own studies so far, only older children could consciously reflect on a process of ego-dissolution as younger children seemed to be "already there". This does not mean that the two states (pre- and post-egoic) are ontologically different, in terms of chthonic and mystical states.

Psychologist Steve Taylor argues that children demonstrate a natural joy and wonder, achieved through the child's openness to the dynamic ground.[89] Gradually, the ego develops and represses or covers the ground. This is different than being separate from the ground of being (or true self) – and implies a return to self rather than a developmental growth towards self. By early adulthood, the ego has alienated from the ground and becomes deprived of its vitality. Self is *felt* as separate. The process of transformation is a reopening to the dynamic ground and reintegration with our being. Taylor suggests that early childhood and the transpersonal spiritual state are not ontologically distinct, only expressed differently in a pre- or transpersonal form. Psycholinguists Jacques Lacan and Julia Kristeva suggest a young child starts to form self-identity with an object that represents himself to himself. An imagined identity emerges where the "I" as an entity comes to the fore with the child identifying with that self-conception.[90] This is a projected identity, an apparent self, from an identity that is prior to the maternal and paternal laws of language and society.

There are debates about whether those who are *enlightened* (a problematic word) can transmit this state of consciousness to others. Informal reports from followers of mystics and gurus suggest this could be the case. What is less noted, is how newborn infants can catalyze a similar transformational process in their own parents. Often, parents can report their own shift to a sense of oneness or deep connectedness, following the birth of their children. Midwives and birth doulas report the unearthly radiance exuded by mothers after a healthy birth, with midwives themselves experiencing transformation.[91] Other prominent figures in education and psychology have noted a transmission type effect from children to adults or between children. Rudolf Steiner created a new form of education for children, known as the "Steiner Education Approach". Steiner saw children has having a participative consciousness, an awareness of the invisible world that allows the child to be nearer to spiritual reality than an adult. While psychologist Edward Edinger notes how the infant is totally identified with self and experiences itself as a deity, provoking adults into a nostalgia about our origins.

My own view, developed from working and researching with children, and from my own experiences as a child, supports the idea that younger children are simply and directly accessing a ground of being (Consciousness), that is always already there regardless of age. Children and adults can return to this state of consciousness or ground at any time. Nature is designed to ensure that in some way, usually through suffering and crisis, we can either take a peek or plunge back into that ground of being. In doing so, children may readily access those mythological dimensions Jung recognizes, accessing different states of consciousness, and experiences of Self, that are referred to as "anomalous", "paranormal", "transpersonal" or "disordered". If self is understood through mainstream ideas, these types of experiences should not be possible.

Exploring Self and Unexplained Experiences with Children

Children and young people have demonstrated accessing a "truer self" in some of the studies I have conducted. In the "Who am 'I'?" study (2019), we (the children and I) explored the nature of "self" and unexplained experiences. Children identified different ways of being or senses of self that appeared to correspond with certain types of unexplained experiences:

Three senses of self: Taken from the "Who am 'I'?" study 2019

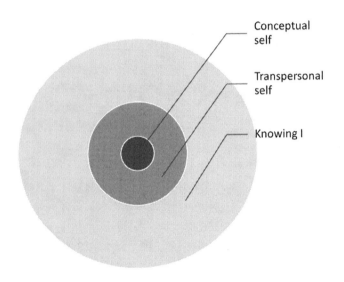

The diagram shows three ways in which children experienced their *self* during the "Who am 'I' Study". The concentric circles show how senses of self are not separate but emerge from a field of self (Knowing I-ness). This is shown through the large circle. The conceptual and transpersonal selves are experienced differently by children while the knowing I (the large circle) appeared to be experienced, by children, in the same way. Children accessed a knowing I in two ways in the study: reporting it as a memory of a peak experience or through a self-enquiry research activity. Some children in the study had spontaneous peak experiences in nature or in hospital. These are experiences where the individual self is dissolved and replaced with an expanded sense of being one with the universe. During the study, children would report these types of experiences and reflect on who they are in peak moments. Children who had these experiences were invited to take part in an activity called "Take a Selfie".

The activity involved children enquiring into the self beyond their sense of individual personhood, using self-enquiry techniques. The idea came from modern non-duality practices, developed by teachers such as Rupert Spira,92 and from the popular youth culture phenomenon of the selfie. In moments when children appeared to be accessing the knowing I, they remained silent, their bodies still. Following their self-enquiry, we explored the sense of self they had experienced in this state. When children were asked to describe this sense of self, they would say, "I don't know but I just know it's the real me." Children described this state of self as timeless. Language could not convey children's experiences and they could only represent "What I am not" (a conceptual self). The smallest circle represents the conceptual self, a sense of being an individual body that experiences others and the world. At this stage of self, children expressed diverse identities, made up of concepts and things (stories, names, schools, friends etc.). Like children, I find it difficult to write about something that cannot be explained in books. The diagram can only point towards how the nature of self may extend far beyond our sense of personhood.

Children's reports about the transpersonal self, emerged when they tried to convey their unexplained experiences. The transpersonal self was made up of other selves (in the form of other people's thoughts, emotions and bodily sensations). Self and experience are shown to be tightly correlated. Unexplained experiences following a peak experience can be intense and frequent, having the potential to destabilize the child if they are not supported in appropriate ways. The types of experiences reported are intense telepathy, frequent OBEs and lucid dreams, past life memories, voice-hearing (sometimes in languages not their own) and premonitions. Experiences, such as peak or mystical, were felt by young people in the hospital (as a surge of deep gratitude) or in nature (powerful feeling/knowing of being one with the environment). Children sensed a transpersonal self when trying to report experiences such as empathic connections, telepathy, premonitions and other, non-local mental experiences. When children reported their experiences, such as engaging with other beings, seeing lights or hearing strange noises, they were more aligned with a conceptual sense of self. There seems to be an interesting relationship between the types of experiences children have and how they experience who they are. When children are told or reminded that they are a separate, limited self, who must achieve or compete with others to find value, suffering arises. When unexplained experiences intrude into conceptual spaces of self, older children and young people can be in conflict between their conditioned ideas about self and reality, and what they are experiencing. The "knowing I" that children experienced and identified as a truer sense of self, me or "I", corresponds with Taylor's dynamic ground, Lacan and Kristeva's "register of the real" and Albahari's "aperspectival witness consciousness" (see chapter 10).

The knowing I-ness of experience demonstrated by children was recognized (by children) as the "real me". In an earlier research study (2018) I conducted with thirty 6-7-year-olds, children recognized an observer self that could witness their inner stories. The activity was conducted in a school context and framed around relationships with others (their peers). Children followed the sound of a single singing bowl note to move into a silent space (this was presented as a game – so not to influence children's experiences). The aim of the game was to place all attention on the sound until it disappeared. Children had to close their eyes (so they would not be distracted) and raise their hand when the sound disappeared. Children reported feeling quiet, peaceful and empty. From this position, children were then asked to enquire into their inner stories about relationships on the playground. I framed the activity to gently steer children away from any other inner narratives that might have arisen as part of the activity (i.e. traumatic stories, stories about other people away from school). Children then used art to represent their inner stories and reauthor them (i.e., "that boy does not like me, he pushed me when playing football" – "I don't like that boy because he accidently hurt me when playing football"). There seems to be more to who we are than meets the eye. Children's unexplained experiences are a vista from which we can understand greater insights into the nature of self and reality. These ideas are explored more in chapter 10.

The Limitations of the Modern "Self" and Unexplained Experiences

Children can suffer when they have unexplained experiences. Suffering does not seem to be created through the experience itself, but by how society responds to these types of experiences. In western culture, "self" is defined in quite limiting ways. The American Psychology Association defines "self" as *"an individual's feeling of identity, uniqueness and self-direction"*. If we look carefully at this assertion, it becomes clear that self is defined as a property of an individual. My own research with children is starting to show how self is experienced beyond these definitions. Other studies with adults that examine transformational experiences; psychedelics and meditation also demonstrate how self extends far beyond mainstream narratives about who we are. Unexplained experiences (and other types of subjective and shared experiences) are often understood from the perspective of an individual self – despite "self" remaining a mystery. Scientists have not found a "self" located in the body/brain. William James referred to "self" as the "puzzling puzzle", a mystery that remains with us today.

The last twenty years have seen a sort of renaissance of ideas about self, as interest in epistemology (knowledge), ontology (what is) and methodology (how we find out) is growing. Not just in science but in the lifeworlds of everyday people who are becoming dissatisfied with expert descriptions about their own experiences and realities. It seems the more we try and understand self and living experience, the more complex it appears to be. Historical ideas about being human are shrouded in the image of man as a rational animal endowed with language.[93] *Man* in this definition has a literal meaning that has historically positioned children, women and communities outside the western world as *other*. You can see the image of the rational man portrayed in Leonardo da Vinci's *Vitruvian Man* and in other forms of Italian Renaissance art. This is a symbol of classical humanism, strongly linked to rationality and humans' relationship to an inert physical world of matter.

Postmodern thought emerged as a challenge to this fixed idea of humanity and the world. Sociologist Anthony Giddens has heavily influenced how identity is understood in social science, as fluid, multiple and discursive. Giddens also noted how human beings need to continuously reaffirm themselves through consumption, by having relationships through a narcissistic fixation with processes such as personal and health development.[94] We see this in the growing self-help industry that appropriates Eastern practices, such as yoga and mindfulness. These activities tend to be marketed through a capitalist ideology. Individual improvement can lead to better performance.

Mindfulness is taught in schools to children, not to encourage self-gnosis (self-enquiry) but to improve grades and attainment levels. Individualism, competition and the deep-rooted adage *survival of the fittest* has meant that we have become seemingly separate from each other and the world around us.

All these ideas shape how children's unexplained experiences are understood in a modern world. What is becoming clear is how children's experiences and how they sense who they are contradict individualism and competition. Children's experiences of self and unexplained phenomena point to a reality whose features are deeply intra-connected, relational yet deep and nonphysical. It's time to cross the bridge into new territories and systems of thought that can offer more explanatory power for children's selves and unexplained experiences. Not for the sake of adding to existing theory but for social transformation. In the next chapter, I consider children's selves and unexplained experiences in the context of states of consciousness.

Chapter 7

Children's Unexplained Experiences and States of Consciousness

I had the weirdest dream. I was in a place, like a city made out of crystal. I was with people I didn't know but I kinda do know them. It wasn't like a dream, it felt real.

Lola, aged 15 years

Children's reports of unexplained experiences, such as invisible friends or travelling to different worlds, are not often taken seriously by adults, scholars and scientists. That may be because children navigate the everyday world through imagination, play and now cyberspace. For adults, reality can be clearly defined by what is logical or possible and shared by many people. And there can be clear instances when a child can miscalculate an illusion, such as mistaking an adult dressed up as a big teddy bear, for an actual big teddy bear. This doesn't mean that children's imaginary worlds or playful activities don't hold some aspect of a reality that goes beyond usual ideas of a fixed, physical reality. Play is a child's activity that is very much taken for granted. Yet very little is known about the nature of play, just as little is known about the nature of consciousness. Social scientists will speculate that play is a socially constructed activity, involving children mimicking adults. Psychologists may note how play helps resolve children's trauma and conflicted emotions. Neuroscientists cannot yet explain play through brain activity. These leave us with the mystery of play and why it is such an integral aspect of children's ways of being and acting in the world.

Play has qualities such as creativity and timelessness, features that can be found in altered states of consciousness. Researchers such as Tanous & Donnelly note how children's imaginary friends should not be so easily dismissed, linking altered states of consciousness such as bi-location, to how children participate in the world. Research studies that show how children's video game playing can initiate lucid dream states, also correspond with these ideas. In this chapter, I explore children's states of consciousness and their relationship to time, space and unexplained experiences. Ways of being that contradict "normal mental functioning"[95] are often referred to as "altered states of consciousness". This is a useful term (like "unexplained") to refer to different sets of experiences and perceptions but implies that there is a normal state of consciousness. Too little is known about the mind and states of consciousness, to affirm one state as normal (often equating to healthy or productive), from which other states are measured against (altered). With this point made, Charles Tart suggests that an altered state of consciousness is a multidimensional phenomenon, where not one aspect of consciousness is affected, but multiple aspects of consciousness are affected in an intense manner. Many psychometric tests and multiple measurement questionnaires have been used to capture the multidimensional features of altered states of consciousness.[96] Understanding children's experiences of self and unexplained phenomena needs to be examined in the context of states of consciousness. I explore this through this chapter. I also examine children's dreams as states of consciousness that can have exceptional features.

Children and Play

Claims that children can fantasize about their unexplained experiences are often linked to the activity of play. For over a century, play research has produced speculation as to why play occurs in children but with little conclusive agreement.[97] Mainstream definitions of play suggest it is a socially constructed activity. Children's creativity is linked to play with scholars in the field suggesting it is a product of the activity of play. I would argue that the impulse to create drives children to play, rather than play causing creativity. As the famous playwright George Bernard Shaw reminds us, we don't stop playing because we grow old, we grow old because we stop playing. Society demands that we stop playing, not just adults but also children, through regimented educational systems that privilege erudite knowledge and practices, above creativity and freedom of expression. Play cuts across species. Baby animals, from vertebrates to invertebrates, engage in play. Even the octopus and the honeybee play. As psychologist Terry Marks-Tarlow notes, play entrains, that is, brings into sync, physiological systems in mother and child along with their underlying brain waves.[98] When children play, they learn to navigate space that helps them weave strands of genetic inheritance with the intersubjective threads of their lives into a fractal tapestry, embodying self in physical and social space – aligning inner vision and outer expression.

The benefits of play have been widely evidenced. Piers & Landau (1980) suggest that play develops feelings of joy and pleasure and the habit of being happy. Play purists argue that play occurs for no real purpose. That depends on how purpose is defined. In mainstream society, purpose is often measured against how one contributes towards society. Play seems to be a necessary process for well-being, as Newson et al show in their studies with disabled children in the seventies. Children who are prevented from usual play (involving lots of movement and sensory experiences) because of their disabilities will experience relative deprivation in terms of sensory experiences.[99] In modern times, this has been addressed through the introduction of sensory rooms for children who cannot engage in the usual active play displayed by children. Different therapeutic practices appeal to play when supporting children. Play during psychotherapy is not viewed as a frivolous activity but instead expands the subjective space allowing for safe exploration. A process familiar to yoga teachers, who frequently guide students to approach the asanas or poses, playfully as a means of creating more space.[100]

Psychoanalytic writers and practitioners view play as a state rather than a functional activity. Donald Winnicott (1896-1971), a pediatric doctor and psychoanalyst, developed the concepts of transitional phenomena and potential space, using them to explain the play state. Winnicott uses the term *transitional* to describe an intermediate play space between inner and outer reality. We could think of other transitional spaces as those experienced during puberty, as a child evolves from one form into another. A transitional object is used to bridge inner and outer worlds. Despite the transitional object being viewed as an external object by an outside observer (mother etc.), Winnicott suggests it is experienced by the infant as being neither self, other, internal or external world – but on the boundary between these, as a point of intersection. Winnicott notes that *"a transitional object is one about which the question 'Is it created by me, or does it come from the outside' cannot meaningfully be asked, because it does not exist in either of these psychic realms."*[101] Children weave objects and others into their own experience and subjectivity. This is often seen as an illusory act (an illusion that we are intra-connected or create our external reality) by Winnicott and in mainstream early years literature. Young children form attachments to external objects to retain a sense of omnipotence or control over reality, a habit that continues throughout life, seen in adult behaviors such as addiction and desire. The illusion, according to Winnicott, is an infant's sense of being omnipotent, creating the external world and perceiving everything as a facet of their own subjectivity. Perhaps the illusion of separation is what young children move into, rather than leaving behind a disillusion of oneness.

Winnicott is referring to an infant's sense of self before ego consciousness emerges, where there is no separation between self, others and the world (like those states discussed in the previous chapter). Altered states of consciousness are often studied with adults, and scholars showing the many different types of altered states of consciousness we naturally shift into in everyday life. Examples include drowsiness, daydreaming, diet, orgasm, respiratory maneuvers, sensory overload, dancing and sleep deprivation. I would add *play* to this long list. Children appear to move into a dissociated state, where usual time, space, bodies and personhood are disrupted through children's own agential acts. This is different to the dissociation reported by older children and young people, who suddenly begin to feel that their person, other people and reality is "not real" or "like a dream". This can distress young people and dissociation has been pathologized in this age group, without fully exploring the phenomenon. Dissociation appears to be a process of suspending a constructed consensual social reality – in older children this doesn't seem to be a conscious choice – whereas young children are evoking a suspension of the "norm" through play.

Play and the Brain

There is limited research in neuroscience that examines brain activity in children when they play and little evidence regarding the neural regions that are active when children are playing. There is a growing body of literature that examines neural activity in adults who are meditators or use psychedelics, activities that induce altered states of consciousness. Surprisingly, studies show a reduction in brain activity when using psychedelics or meditating, despite people having rich conscious experiences.[102] The research conducted by neuroscientists[103] has implications for how we understand the function of the brain – not as a producer of our experiences but perhaps as a reducing valve that limits our perception of reality.

Dopamine is a widely studied neurotransmitter that has been linked to well-being. High levels of dopamine are said to induce motivation, goal directedness, exploratory behavior, reward prediction, working memory and creativity.[104] Dopamine is also linked to play in children and animals. The complexity of play does not depend on the size of an animal's brain. For example, octopi can use their water jets to push floating objects back and forth in a tank or in a circular path, despite their brains being half the diameter of a dime. Animals' play behaviors are linked to rises in dopamine and it seems so due to altered states of consciousness in human beings. Studies show how meditation practice increases dopamine. One study found a 65% increase in levels of dopamine, in a part of the brain called the striatum as people practice yoga nidra (a meditative state halfway between sleep and waking).[105] Humans who are prone to seek altered states of consciousness may best be explained by the high dopamine content of the human brain, which orientates us to extra personal space, a common denominator of all ASC.[106] Play is a natural state of consciousness, a bridge opening the child to nonmaterial, liminal spaces that involves minds and bodies. Play, whether on video games, in parks or in private spaces, evokes a state in which children are reconnecting, communicating and co-creating with the unseen.

Rituals and States of Consciousness

In the past, the Puritans viewed playing as sinful. Yet the art of play is featured in the Christian and Jewish scriptures with most translations using the words *rejoicing* instead of *play*. In the Hebrew bible, rejoicing means to play.[107] References to play and the presence of the divine can be found in the Hebrew scriptures:

I was at his side, a master craftsman
Delighting him (God) day after day
Ever at play in his presence
At play everywhere in the world
Ecclesiastes 2:10, 3:12

In early religious scripture, play is synonymous with a joyful state of presence. The literature around altered states of consciousness refers to this as *transcendence* or states of oneness. Play in its deepest form entails a transcendence of the *norm*, a mystical state of consciousness from which different expressions, such as freedom, happiness, connectedness and creativity emerge. In play as a transcendental realm, distinctions between self and others, the material and immaterial collapse, similar with the ego-dissolution experiences of adults – or the mystical experiences defined by scholars such as William James or Abraham Maslow.

In his book *The Varieties of Religious Experience*, William James (1896) promoted a radical empiricism, declaring that "personal religious experience has its root and center in mystical states of consciousness."[108] This means that human experience was highly valued by James, as he claimed many religious ideas may have come from the experiences people have in altered states of consciousness. James noted how ritual and play induced *transmarginal consciousness*, states of consciousness that are subtly veiled in the everyday. There are many rituals involved in religious practices such as lighting incense, drinking wine and eating bread. Shamans will dance, sing and beat the drum so they can travel through states of consciousness to bring wisdom and healing to the whole community. Trance has been linked to ritual and play by William James and contemporary writers such as Jay Mechling and Roger Caillois.

In *Man, Play and Games* (1958), Roger Caillois suggested different categories of gameplay. One class of play is referred to as *ilinx*, the Greek word for *whirlpool*. Ilinx is a type of trance state, "an attempt to momentarily destroy the stability of perception and inflict a kind of voluptuous panic upon an otherwise lucid mind… surrendering to a kind of spasm, seizure or shock which destroys reality with a sovereign brusqueness."[109] In children, this may be seen in spinning around until they fall over in fits of laughter or moving in great rotations on playground equipment. In adult ritual, this may be seen in the whirling dervishes or the parachuter hurtling to earth from the plane. In *Children's Folklore: A Handbook* (2008), Elizabeth Tucker discusses dangerous play, in the form of nonsexual choking games played by children, that are similar to adult and adolescent versions of asphyxiation. Children enjoy this form of play because of the ecstatic feelings associated with oxygen deprivation. It becomes clear that there are many natural and subtle ways that children enter into enhanced states of consciousness that could catalyze experiences considered unexplained.

Children and Time

Children have a taste for the chaotic and unknown. In play, children seek loss of control and uncertainty as they push beyond boundaries. Some scholars believe children are preparing themselves for a chaotic world, others suggest links to self-regulation cognitive and linguistic left-brain competencies, within a developing child. Children may be seeking to connect with the unknown, timeless and unbounded, rather than emulate grown-ups in a chaotic world. The connections between altered states of consciousness and time have been well documented in recent psychology literature. Research with adults shows how experiences of *normal* time can be expanded through activities such as extreme sports and meditation practices. Negative states such as PTSD and trauma can also create an experience of time slowing down. Tachypsychia is the medical term used to describe a rupture in how normal time is experienced, used to explain both a contraction and/or an expansion of time. Normal time is often associated with clocks, routines and the calendar and is how we perceive our movements through the world, as linear and chronological. Language supports this perception, crafted to describe and construct linear time through words, tenses and other linguistic markers, that give rise to a sense of moving through a passage of time. Young children don't experience time in this way, as chronological time emerges from ego-consciousness (conditioning, separation, abstract thinking about the future etc.). This may explain why time appears to speed up as we grow older. As children meet the world through new experiences and sensory processing, rather than the abstract and conceptual way adults do, the present moment is all there is.

Time is still a mystery to scientists. Einstein suggested that we live in a block universe, where there is no linear progression of time. Time, according to Einstein, is like elastic that contorts and is relative to speed and mass. Theoretical physicist Carlo Rovelli, in his book *The Order of Time*, sees time as an illusion. A naïve perception we share that doesn't correspond with reality. Rovelli makes some interesting claims about time, such as the flow of time is a subjective feature of the universe and not an objective part of the world. It is not a thing that we are in, rather time is affected by the observer. These new ideas about time can support how children's states of consciousness, normally defined as altered, or out of normal time, could constitute natural ways of being. Children in my own studies who have experienced a mystical or peak experience often describe how time does not exist during their experiences. In my own experience as a child, time as we understand it seemed to collapse. When children try to describe interactions with deceased people or events in hypnogogic states, time seems to be spatial rather than linear. Experiences of time corresponded with children's experiences of self. When children reported conventional experiences (attending school, names and ages etc.), their reports characterize time as moving in a straight line. When children reported unexplained experiences, their reporting strategies became nonlinear, non-linguistic and metaphorical (using a concrete idea to represent something abstract/unexplainable). References to time are often made by children when reporting unusual dreams. Time can be erratic and spatial, cease to exist or slow down.

Children's Exceptional Dreams

In Shakespeare's *The Tempest*, the magician Prospero claims, "we are such stuff that dreams are made on, and our little life is rounded with a sleep." Through Prospero, Shakespeare alludes to the idea that waking life is like a dream. Similar ideas about reality can be found in ancient texts, that suggest waking reality is a type of Maya (illusion). Scientists still have no real answers about dreams or why they happen. Dreams are often thought of as brain activity that re-represent our daily activities or unconscious patterns in the psyche. In ancient times, people would visit dream temples and incubate dreams for healing and wisdom. In some First Nation communities, dreams are considered an important part of culture, used for initiation and transition to other states of being. Native American and Aboriginal cultures see dreams as doorways to worlds that go beyond conventional reality.

Nearly all children I speak or research with describe strange or lucid dream states that they have frequently. In my own studies, lucid and otherworldly dreams rank statistically as the most common type of unexplained experience. This may correspond with children's frequent ventures into virtual realities. Dreams are not considered unexplained; they are accepted in mainstream society and can be discussed openly without stigma. Yet children have dreams that are very "real" to them and have qualities of experiences such as premonitions, mediumship, travelling to other realities and lucidity in dream states. These are known as exceptional dreams by scholars such as Fariba Bogzaran, Stanley Krippner & Daniel Deslauriers. During the lockdown, children and adults reported a higher incidence of dreaming activity. In my own research (during the lockdown), I noted more teenagers than younger children reporting lucid and shared dreams. Like unexplained experiences, dreams have been organized by scholars into types. Bogzaran suggests there are precognitive or transcendent dreams (where dreamers have a direct experience of ego dissolution). Dreams have the potential to affect how we interact with the world in waking consciousness. For example, professionals can rehearse and enhance their skills through lucid dream training.

Examples of children's dreams that I have collated include visiting scenes from past lives, travelling through crystalline cities and being given information (that is often forgotten but the child knows it is there) and meeting deceased relatives. Some children have reported premonitions through dreams while others have travelled through the universe and different star constellations. Dreams can be considered as states of consciousness that can teach us about the nature of the reality that we engage in each day. Carl Jung saw dreams as "the smallest hidden door in the deepest and most inner sanctum of the soul which opens into that primeval cosmic night that was long before there was a conscious ego."[110] I discuss Jung in more detail in the next chapter that considers children's unexplained experiences and the collective consciousness.

Chapter 8

Children and the Collective Consciousness

Are you, are you comin' to the tree
Where I told you to run so we'd both be free?
Strange things did happen here, no stranger would it be
If we met at midnight in the hanging tree
Katniss, *The Hunger Games*

The Hunger Games is a novel and film, set in a dystopian future. The world Suzanne Collins has created in her trilogy, sees a nation divided following a great rebellion of the twelve districts that exist to serve the "Capitol" and its luxurious lifestyle. As punishment for the rebellion, there is a reaping, with each district mandated to enter two of their children into a lottery. The children will then fight each other to the death, in a glorified Reality-TV-type event. Children are being punished for the ancestral mistakes of adults, and order is maintained through the districts to avoid further rebellion. The Capitol maintains its power through wealth, and narratives that sustain the idea that "the reaping" is for the benefit of the whole. Districts have become so accustomed to the reaping they no longer question it. Katniss is the young female protagonist, "a girl on fire with a philosopher's love of truth"[111] – who through her compassion, courage and critical intuition, slowly strips away the layers of adult deceit that create the dystopian world of Panem. The popularity of the book and movie among teenagers is sparked by the archetypal presence of Katniss, who embodies spontaneity while craving normality, bravery while incredibly vulnerable, rebellious while seeking a new world order. Katniss is a young person, among many others in the story, that must transcend the internal and external realities formed collectively by adults of the past. *The Hunger Games* is a social story that hints at the unconscious collective patterns that normalize and sustain the appalling ritual of the games. Perhaps an exaggerated metaphor for how modern children may be affected by a collective consciousness, informed and fed by adults from the past and present day.

This chapter takes the ideas formulated in earlier chapters and starts to think about how children may interact with each other in subtle spaces beyond our "physical" world. I consider children's unexplained experiences (telepathy, PK etc.) and other experiences (such as OCD; birth) within different theories proposed by scholars in the fields of psychiatry and psychology. Thinkers and practitioners, such as Carl Jung, Marie-Louise von Franz, Christina Grof and Stanislav Grof, and Rupert Sheldrake, propose a field of collective mental activity or transpersonal realms that interpenetrate the lifeworlds of everyday people. The work of these scholars has historically been relegated to pseudo-science, disrespected and disregarded by an academic system that privileges research in accordance with their own ideologies and agendas. My own view is that fields such as mainstream psychiatry and psychology will soon need to accommodate theories like the ones proposed in this chapter. Especially when everyday people are becoming more resistant to mainstream psychiatric explanations about their selves and experiences.

Children and Mind Patterns

In all my years of researching with children, I've noticed how often they will discuss repetitive and unusual mind patterns or "sticky thoughts". What is interesting about their thoughts is that they either fall into significant categories, such as violent thoughts or religiosity; or they reveal information that the child should not be aware of (i.e., events from the past). Many children are taken to see a medical doctor when these thoughts become problematic. The mainstream label for them is OCD (obsessive compulsive thought disorder). OCD refers to a phenomenon where people experience intrusive and repetitive thoughts. Sometimes, this can affect the behaviors of children, leading to actions such as repetitive handwashing or counting toys repeatedly. In severe cases, OCD can be debilitating, having significant impacts on everyday life. Obsessive compulsive disorder (OCD) is a growing phenomenon among young children and teenagers that affected 1-2% of the population in the early 2000s, increasing to 2-3% in 2015. It is estimated that this number would be significantly higher if people reported their experiences of OCD. The average onset of OCD is 6-11 years with a mean age of 10.3 years (although there are increased reports of younger children having severe OCD symptoms).

Despite the DSM-5 stating that OCD is a neuropsychiatric disorder, health professionals do not know what OCD *is*. There is still a very limited understanding of OCD's pathophysiology, although there are recent attempts to identify the circuits that are thought to underlie complex repetitive behaviors.[112] Neuroscientists are attempting to explain OCD by examining circuit dysfunction in the brain. OCD is diagnosed in children as young as five, by using evidence-based assessment – a list of measures developed from other people reporting similar internal experiences. In a 2006 paper, Friedlander & Desrocher undertook a comprehensive review of OCD neuroimaging studies, looking at possible correlations with executive dysfunction and modulatory control (sets of cognitive processes, such as attention and memories, that are linked to certain areas of the brain). The authors noted that findings are not consistent in OCD, with research into OCD only examining correlations between OCD symptoms and neural activity. To date, there is no exact cognitive profile for OCD in children and no real explanations for this common phenomenon. A recent systematic review of the literature in 2020, found that children presented with robust increases in brain error related negativity, associated with certain cognitive processes (abnormal action motoring, impaired decision-making). Scans can show how larger than normal waveforms, in certain areas of the brain, are the same as those detected during acute alcohol usage.[113] According to neuroscientific studies, the *intoxication state of consciousness*[114] that is there when drinking alcohol is found to be there in children experiencing OCD thought patterns.

What is interesting about OCD is that all people (children and adults) who report it experience one or several common thought-pattern themes. These are thoughts that are entangled in certain grand themes or narratives. These themes are judgement, ideas of damnation (religiosity), self-punishment, sexually explicit thoughts, and violent thoughts. Very young children are reporting intrusive and obsessive thoughtforms that fit into one or several of these categories. OCD is also a common symptom of autism, psychosis and ADHD – some of the most identified conditions attributed to children. Instead of exploring the nature of these thoughts and associated themes, children are quickly diagnosed and often treated with medication, in closed clinical contexts. What is evident, is that OCD appears to be a habitual mind pattern which children (and adults) have no control over.

As a researcher who explores all kinds of experiences with children, my first question is: how do very young children experience intrusive and persistent thought patterns that pertain to grand, shared and collective human themes? Some may argue that it's down to sociocultural influences from bad parents, scary movies and social media. If this was the case, we would expect a wider range of content, not specific themes. Children from all different cultures, socioeconomic backgrounds and different walks of life experience the same phenomenon. Many of these younger children have not been exposed to such content. It doesn't explain the sheer force of these patterns which break into the developing ego-consciousness of children.

Pre-existing patterns or forms that can shape our experiences have been noted by thinkers such as Plato and Carl Jung and can be found in literary classics. The seven deadly sins are thought to represent these pre-existing forms, found in Dante's *Inferno* and Chaucer's *Canterbury Tales*. The seven deadly sins have their origins in a discovery made by a monk in the 4th century. Writer and teacher, Evagrius Ponticus travelled into the Egyptian desert to join a monastery. During meditation, Ponticus noted eight evil thoughts (Gluttony, Lust, Avarice, Dejection, Anger, Listlessness, Vanity and Pride). These evil, persistent and intrusive thoughts now represent the infamous seven deadly sins. It seems that pre-existing thoughtforms have been noted throughout history. Children often claim their thoughts as their own, feeling shame or distress and believing they are "evil". This can feed intrusive thought patterns and ritualistic behaviors, such as repeated handwashing. As Rupert Sheldrake notes, rituals are where social memory is invoked in cultural and religious contexts, across all societies. For example, Christians drink the blood and eat the body of Jesus through the ingestion of wine and bread. It seems possible that children may be tapping into (perhaps not through their individual volition) a non-local collective field, like those proposed by thinkers such as Carl Jung, Marie-Louise von Franz and Stanislav & Christina Grof.

Children and the Collective Unconscious

The thematic material of OCD can also link with Carl Jung's ideas about the deeper forces that invade the personal psyche – known as the archetypes. Jungian psychology focuses on the depths of the unconscious mind, those aspects of our self that we cannot easily access. Marie-Louise von Franz, a student of Carl Jung, devoted her life's work to understanding the nature of the autonomy of this collective aspect of the psyche. According to Jung and von Franz, the collective unconscious contains objective experiences that are outside our control. This seems to correspond with how children (and adults) experience the phenomenon OCD, as intrusive and out of their control. It could explain much more, for example how we may be predisposed to certain desires, repulsions and behaviors. Jung proposes how some of these objective experiences can cross the boundary, entering the ego, producing discernible effects. The background of the unconscious continuously influences ego-consciousness. As younger children are already in the process of ego-development, their boundaries may be more porous and open to the contents of a collective unconscious. Jung asserted that children's closeness to the collective unconscious meant that their awareness of its contents is greater than adults.

The important point Jung makes is that the unconscious is collective and transpersonal, structured by archetypal patterns of psychic activity, that influence our thoughts, feelings and actions.[115] Jung suggests that archetypal patterns are not acquired but are innate, like instincts. For example, the child archetype contains features such as playfulness, spontaneity, innocence, creativity and vibrance. In the modern world children and adults cannot express the child archetype due to the rigid, institutional, rule-governed nature of society. Jungian psychologist Erich Neumann notes how well-being depends on the functioning and balance of archetypal material. If adults are suppressing or ignoring archetypal forces, or those aspects of ourselves that we would rather not see, perhaps our children are feeling the effects of our collective ignorance.

Sigmund Freud still heavily influences how children are understood in modern times. His contemporary, Carl Jung, has not had as much influence (although in recent times, Jung's theories are becoming more popular). Neither Freud nor Jung focused specifically on children, yet childhood theories formed their different psychologies.[116] Freud suggested that adult neurosis was a product of sexual repression, positioning children as "polymorphously perverse."[117] Jung's growing distaste for Freud's construction of children forced a further move away from his former mentor's theories. Jung wrote about children in an abstract way, using the child archetype as a means for identifying the rich symbolic and imaginary lives of children. Jung used examples of stories told by children which expressed life events, such as babies being born. Stories of angel-storks and reincarnation were for Jung a positive expression of the psyche rather than Freud's repressed sexuality. For Jung it was an expression of how children participate in the mysterious, numinous quality of human experience.[118]

Jung noted that children have a unique relationship with the collective unconscious, by virtue of their lack of differentiation from it – suggesting children do not have an individual psyche before ego development.[119] According to Jung, the child is fused with the psyche of earlier generations (ancestors), with grandparents and great-grandparents who are the true progenitors.[120] The child's individual psyche, according to Jung, is only a potential, existing in a state of *participation mystique* with his/her ancestors – and the collective unconsciousness, with its transpersonal, universal and inherited nature. The collective unconscious plays an integral role in child development, with the ego emerging from it – seen through the child's developing awareness of the *I*. Although Jung posited the ego as central to personhood (personality consciousness), it does not constitute the "Self". The role of the ego, according to Jung, is to veil the contents of the collective unconscious, through a process of differentiation or dissociation. Jung makes a distinction between the collective unconscious and collective consciousness that we see played out in the social world. As children grow, dissociating from the collective unconsciousness, children's selves are shaped more by the collective consciousness (narratives, practices, language etc.).

Fetuses, Adults and the Prenatal and Transpersonal Realms

Jung saw birth as an archetypal reality, embodying the essential patterns of human experience that are known and lived through one's own birth experience; uroboric containment, fall and separation, existential impotence and despair, conflict and struggle, emergent hope and transformative deliverance.[121] Through their research studies with thousands of adults, psychiatrist Stanislav Grof and his late wife Christina Grof demonstrated how the process of birth involves a re-encounter with the ground of the collective unconscious. Grof writes, "during episodes of undisturbed embryonal existence, we typically have experiences of vast regions with no boundaries or limits. We can identify with galaxies, interstellar space or the entire cosmos."[122] Grof & Grof suggest that adult mystical experiences recapture this pre-transpersonal state in a mature form, challenging the early pre-fallacy hypothesis of Ken Wilber (discussed in earlier chapters). From their experiments with thousands of adults, Grof & Grof designed a cartography of the psyche, claiming the mainstream view of the psyche is painfully inadequate. Two additional domains are mapped onto the psyche by Grof, the prenatal and the transpersonal.

The prenatal realm corresponds with the trauma of biological birth and a region of consciousness that contains fetal memories of physical and emotional experiences from the consecutive birth stages (contractions, moving through the birth canal, birth). These memories are mapped by Grof as Basic Perinatal Matrices (BPM I-IV), each of them representing an opening into the areas of the historical and archetypal collective unconscious – which contain motifs of similar experiential qualities. For example, they refer to cases of adults who have intense claustrophobia, linking this back to the experience of contractions in the womb. Where the fetus is compressed, with no room for escape. This, according to reports from experiencers, can link to past life memories in the womb of being buried alive. Once adults have relived their prenatal experiences, Grof & Grof report astounding healing outcomes, even for severe conditions such as schizophrenia.

The transpersonal realm is a psychic domain that, according to Grof, harbors mythological figures, themes and realms of all the cultures and ages, even those of which we have no intellectual knowledge. This description resonates with Jung's collective unconscious and archetypal material. Grof notes how fetuses access the transpersonal realms at key transactional birth stages. I have referred to the contraction stage above, experienced as frightening and eternal (as reported by adults who have returned to this stage through psychedelics and holotropic breathwork). Peak and mystical experiences are connected to the final stages of birth when the fetus is released from the confines of the contracting womb. Children do not come into the world as blank slates, as proposed by Freud, rather, a world of collective phenomena is accessed by children before they come into the world. Unexplained experiences of children do carry features of otherworldly artefacts in the form of beings, sounds and voices. Theories such as Grof's and Jung's propose nonmaterial realities there prior to birth and beyond death. How children relate to nonmaterial realities may have something to do with their ways of being, that are not as concretized as adults. Appealing to a collective consciousness that is prior to our physical and conceptual selves offers affordances to understand children's unexplained experiences in new ways. If we are exposed to and carry through contents of a collective consciousness prior to birth, it is logical that children would have certain types of unexplained experiences (such as memories of past lives, access to collective grand themes, information and wisdom beyond their usual capacities etc.). Other types of phenomena such as xenoglossia could also be understood. This is when children spontaneously speak in a language different to their own. Children may be accessing a pre-existing field of knowledge one that is collective in nature.

Into the Field with Children

Progressing the idea of children's close relationship with a collective consciousness (including both unconscious and conscious aspects) gives rise to other questions. The enquiry moves towards the how – meaning, what may be the processes and substance that gives rise to or holds ancestral material, such as thoughts, symbols and images? Rupert Sheldrake proposes that our minds extend beyond our physical brains, as an extension of our everyday experiences. This can be evidenced through phenomena such as knowing when someone is staring at you from behind and turning round to find someone staring; or knowing that it is your friend calling you when your phone starts to ring. This is possible, according to Sheldrake, through a process of morphic resonance. Minds are nonphysical systems of fields that can access collective memories. This morphic field shapes our bodies and other organisms, through a resonance between DNA-transcribed proteins and the morphic field. Sheldrake suggests nature is not fixed by *laws* but is sustained through *habits*. Morphic fields contain inherent memory, the influence of similar patterns of activity in self-organizing systems, across time and space. Each species has a collective memory, given through morphic resonance – a connection from past to present systems across space and time and on the basis of similarity.[123] Memories, according to Sheldrake, are not stored in the brain, rather they are encoded in the morphic fields, out of time. Recalling past events would involve tuning into the corresponding aspects of the morphic field, giving us access to memories across time.

Morphic resonance could in part explain how children access knowledge outside their own belief systems and living experiences. For example, children who report past life memories, could be accessing a collective memory that resonates with their own field, like thought pools. Social and cultural aspects of morphic fields and morphic resonance are proposed by Sheldrake. Societies have social and cultural fields:

> *a familiar comparison might be to that of a hive of bees or a nest of termites: each is like a giant organism, and the insects within it are like cells in a superorganism. Although comprised of hundreds and hundreds of individual insect cells, the hive or nest functions and responds as a unified whole.*
>
> Rupert Sheldrake (2008)

Morphic fields, according to Sheldrake, are within and around the things to which they refer; with the field organizing and coordinating its aspects, "just as the morphic field of the human body coordinates the activities and movements of the cells and tissues and organs."[124] This implies a collective social consciousness that runs deeper than discursive or relational connectivity. Sheldrake suggests the in-built memory of morphic fields helps to explain how certain features of society such as traditions and customs are retained, despite the continuous turnover of individuals. Turning to patterns of nature, what is already available to us can support a theory of morphic resonance. Animals demonstrate a morphic resonance, especially birds who move in perfect synchronicity or the perfect coordinated movements of a school of fish. At its core, morphic resonance explains the habits of nature as memory, locating humans and other living beings, in intra-connected ways, within patterns and flows of nature.

Psychiatrist, Victor Petrenko, proposes an intuitive theory of memory may be needed to understand how people access information beyond usual time and space. As noted earlier, many children seem to access knowledge such as languages, information and mind patterns, which extend beyond their selves and experiences. In a recent article[125] Petrenko draws on theories about intuition and the nature of self (as outside temporal space and time) to suggest the idea of a historical memory of all events and deeds of humanity. Petrenko proposes that genetic memory of humanity could be accessed through various states of consciousness, such as meditation. Self-gnosis may be the key to perform *mental archaeology*. If children are closer to a self that transcends temporal time and space, there may be a natural intuition towards the contents of a genetic field of memory. Explaining how intrusive content such as thoughts and images and memories of other lives could invade children's personal fields.

Petrenko appeals to links between quantum physics and Jung's collective unconscious. Everyday consciousness is object-orientated – where the unconscious has no spatial or temporal coordinates. Evidence of quantum entanglement means that there is no object in the universe that is separate and independent. While no objects are separate, they are demarcated through how we experience them. For example, how we experience contents of our minds is different from how we experience matter. The relationship between mind and matter has been widely debated and referred to as the mind-body problem. Models that propose a shared non-local field of mind can help to explain why children may experience mental phenomena, but how might it explain, for example, how children have birthmarks which correspond with the injury of the person they claim to be in a previous life? This brings us to the mind-body problem which I explore, through children's experiences, in the next chapter.

Chapter 9

Medical Conditions and Unexplained Experiences of Children

I went to the doctors and he was like well you've not got anemia or bad circulation or anything so we don't know, well obviously it's nothing medical so it must be something else. When people don't believe in certain things it's like hard to talk to them about it (unexplained experiences) cause they're like oh don't be silly.
Emma, aged 17 years

Children may be accessing experiences from a collective field, that corresponds to their states of consciousness and unexplained experiences. But what about the body? Making connections between minds and minds entails a smoother step than trying to explain connections between minds and matter. Ian Stevenson's book *Where Reincarnation and Biology Intersect* shows how children's birthmarks correspond with their past life memories (as touched on in earlier chapters). Children would report events from previous lives, including how they died. Their birthmark or defect would match the injury of the deceased person (of who the child claimed to be in a previous life). Stevenson notes that having corresponding birthmarks and defects are important as they provide more objective evidence for reincarnation than just memory. Photographs and post-mortem reports from deceased persons provide interesting data that show significant links between the child's memory and actual events. The data also raises questions about the relationship between mind, body and reality. How is it that the imprint of injuries sustained by one person at a point in time can manifest in the body of a child at another point in time – with the added mystery of the same child accessing the memories of the deceased person?

The wealth of data that Stevenson has generated has astoundingly been ignored by mainstream academia and social/ health policy research. One reason is how the idea of reincarnation entails a reality that is contradictory towards dominant scientific narratives. Children with medical conditions that affect the body and brain can experience unexplained phenomena (past life experiences, having visions, hearing voices and sounds etc.). Some children involved in my own studies have been diagnosed with conditions such as epilepsy, narcolepsy and a relatively new condition called PANS/PANDAS (Pediatric Autoimmune Neuropsychiatric Disorder). What these conditions all have in common is how they can affect regions of the brain, usually through inflammation. Historical studies have made some links between brain abnormalities in children and psychic experiences. One such case was a research study conducted by a Californian psychologist in the early 1970s, Eloise Shields. Shields' research was conducted in a school for children with disabilities. Shields notes the relationship between brain impairment and telepathy in children aged between 7-21 years:

> It appears [these children] can display amazing degrees of telepathy and somewhat above average clairvoyance... these children lack inhibition in speech and behavior and are at an early stage of language development.
> Shields (1970)

Shields considers the striking rapport between groups of children in her study despite their communication difficulties (delayed speech development etc.). The children in Shields' study had experienced damage to their brains through illnesses such as meningitis and injuries sustained through birth. They had a significant reduction or impairment in brain activity.

In this chapter, I examine the links between different medical conditions and children's unexplained experiences, in relation to the mind-body problem. I use the word *condition* with care, associating its meaning with biological issues that impact the lives of children. For example, some children in my research studies have been diagnosed with narcolepsy or epilepsy. Unlike a condition such as autism, both these conditions are identified through significant alterations in biology. For example, narcolepsy will be diagnosed following lumbar punctures and brain scans that will detect a decrease in a spinal fluid chemical. Autism, for example, is mainly diagnosed through clinical diagnostic variables (behavioral characteristics) with no link to a biological correlation. Other illnesses that create inflammation in the body, such as PANS/PANDAS (Pediatric Autoimmune Neuropsychiatric Disorder), coalesce with unexplained experiences. The media refer to PANS/PANDAS as "The Possession Syndrome" and this will be gently examined through the chapter. Research studies that examine inherited trauma (epigenetics) show how children can experience their ancestors' traumatic memories through genetics. Distressing experiences that imprint into minds and bodies may have some bearing on the mystery of birthmarks and past life memories in children.

PANS/PANDAS and Children's Unexplained Experiences

There is a relatively new condition that is on the increase in children and young people, seen mainly in Europe and the US. PANS/PANDAS or Pediatric Autoimmune Neuropsychiatric Disorder is a condition that has been identified largely by parents and groups of medical professionals. Organizations are fighting for the condition to be recognized by governing health bodies and other professionals who work with children. It's important to consider why parents are demanding support and medical care for their children, and what this strange condition entails. Parental anecdotes and media reporting of PANS/

PANDAS refer to it as "The Possession Syndrome". When a *normal* healthy child suddenly "changes over night", following a short-term illness such as tonsilitis or strep throat, parents and carers are left frightened and bewildered. Children suddenly report hearing voices, having visions (people, lights, objects), repetitive intrusive thoughts, regression back to a younger self (toddler status), and other types of experiences that mark a drastic and sudden change in the child. Inflammation in the body and brain is viewed as the primary cause for these experiences and behaviors in children, that can come and go just as quickly (these are known as a flare).

Many of the experiences that children with PANS/PANDAS have carry similar features to the unexplained experiences of children mentioned throughout the book. The difference is how children change overnight in PANS/PANDAS. These changes are linked to their personalities, behaviors (such as aggression) and perceptions. It is the sudden onset and rapid transformation of the child combined with the strong link to common childhood illnesses that sets it apart from other conditions. The two children with PANS/PANDAS in my studies did not experience the extremities of experiences described here. One child (aged 8 years) demonstrated sudden changes with some negative experiences (seeing strange beings). Another child (aged 6 years) became overwhelmed with thoughts, feelings, sensations and perception of others (emphatic tendencies). Online research revealed the range of unexplained experiences of children, from seeing lights, hearing strange music and voice-hearing. PANS/ PANDAS experiences appear to be on a spectrum ranging from mild to severe. PANS/PANDAS draws attention to the interplay between mind and body and the link between viral causes on the body and unexplained experiences that are often negative in nature. The media are responsible for terming PANS/PANDAS as the "possession syndrome", using parents' reports about how their "child is possessed" or "I want my child back" and

"My child went to bed that night and woke up as a completely different person." Staying with parents' observations rather than the media's sensationalism of this condition, I wanted to consider how PANS/PANDAS might be similar to *possessional states*, as defined through the anthropological literature. Before entering this discussion, it's important to note that I am not claiming children are *possessed by an entity*. Rather, I am aiming to tease out the complicated nature of experiences referred to as possession, while exploring how little we know about the mind and body. The reader can decide for themselves how they wish to understand this unusual phenomenon.

Mail Online

'Possessed' schoolboy, eight, held a knife to his throat and told his parents he wanted to 'sit outside until he froze to death' after a THROAT INFECTION triggered outbursts and tics

- [name of child] 'changed overnight' in January 2018
- He told his parents he wanted to die and didn't deserve friends
- It escalated; he would have outbursts of barking and saying suicidal thoughts
- After four months he was diagnosed with PANDAS and put on antibiotics

Spirit possession is a common phenomenon in some First Nation communities – associated with traumatic experiences and usually classified as dissociative disorders.[126] Studies conducted in Uganda with 119 patients show how patients reported partial or full recovery after treatment by traditional healers. Medical treatment conducted on two-thirds of the patients were shown as unsuccessful. During traditional healing sessions, possessing agents were summoned to identify themselves and issues were addressed such as neglect of rituals, issues with ancestors, grief, land conflicts and witchcraft.[127] The authors theorize possessional states as trauma-related dissociation, suggesting trauma-related events such as civil wars could account for the high incidence of people experiencing possession states. An article published in 2012 found that 8% of a population of 1,113 young people, former child soldiers, in Northern Uganda suffered from severe forms of spirit possession.[128] A local variant of spirit possession, known as *cen*, was afflicting the young population. The authors note psychopathology indicators such as PTSD, depression, suicide risk, physical complaints and aggression. *Cen* was more common among former child soldiers, related strongly to extreme levels of traumatic events. Dissociation from an executive or ego self and altered states of consciousness were common factors in possessional experiences. A study carried out in 2010 found that possession is more common than formerly assumed. A war-affected region in Mozambique reported possession experiences, related to impairments of physical health and correlated with trauma-related nightmares.[129]

Individuals and communities can have very clear ideas about their own experiences of possession. Possession can be explained in different ways, depending on the cultural influences of experiencers. There is no clear definition of possession and it is largely viewed as a *thing* that happens, involving the person becoming displaced by a spiritual entity. According to anthropologist Erika Bourguignon (1976), who studied possession in 488 different societies, possession can occur either in a trance or everyday waking state – both which entail the belief that a person is changed through a power "other than the personality, soul, self or the like."[130] Bourguignon noted how affected individuals enter into different states of consciousness. Other explanations of possession involve some form of universal force, that is also an aspect of the affected person, taking executive control. There are various ways that possession is understood and no clear consensus on its nature. Etzel Cardeña in 1989 wrote about varieties of possession, noting the sheer presence of the phenomenon and how it challenges the basic premise of how we conceive of ourselves. Possession, according to Cardeña, is based on something all humans share – a nervous system and body. According to Bourguignon, spirit possession is dependent on the possibility of separating the self from the body. The person is often represented as leaving the body while being replaced by another entity. The whole notion of possession relies on ideas that we are an individual entity and the dual notion that the mind and body are separate things.

If we consider children's experiences of self from earlier chapters, it is obvious that subjects, agents and bodies are not clear cut. Until there is more clarity around the nature of self and mind, a phenomenon such as possession is difficult to define. Modern anthropologists, such as Emma Cohen, suggest that possession states can carry universal features across different cultural contexts. Rather than trance states being the common denominator, Cohen suggests possession as a complex series of patterns of thinking and behavior. Regardless of cultural histories, recurrent features of possession are linked to cognitive architecture that is responsible for perceptions, representations, thoughts and actions. How would complex mental processes outside the executive ego take control of the body? This calls for deeper questions about the substance of mind and matter, as possession necessitates mental processes affecting material bodies. Links between the external environment and a collective consciousness (issues with ancestors) are identified in studies on possession. Traumatic experiences may be linked to distressing types of possessional states, as the literature is starting to show. Children in the countries mentioned here undergo significant traumatic events (such as war). Intense suffering can rupture the boundaries of an executive ego, sometimes leading to peak experiences but not always (as discussed in earlier chapters).

Voice-hearing is another type of experience that feels external to the executive ego. A young person I interviewed with medical conditions described her voice-hearing experiences, that stopped at the age of nine years:

> Usually in your head you just hear your own voice talking but it wasn't mine. So, I think a lot of the time, even though it (the voices) were comforting, I was confused and didn't have control over it.

Cassie had no volition over voices that she *knew* were not her own. I gently explored this further with Cassie, asking if the voices felt outside her sense of personhood. Cassie adamantly stated the voices were external to her. Later, Cassie describes the confusion as a response to discovering not all children hear voices inside their head that are not their own. It is interesting that the voices stopped as Cassie grew older. As our enquiry deepened, Cassie reflected on the *self* she identified with in relation to the voices. Cassie recognized (through several other experiences, including one peak experience) that the *me* or *I* she refers to extends beyond her sense of personhood. This brings us back to the concept of *entity*. We can assume that I am an entity, or you are an entity. But when the idea of an entity is deconstructed, we are left with an assemblage of personal narratives, thoughts, feelings, sensations (body) and perceptions; that are highly conditioned. This is an important point when figuring phenomena such as hearing voices or *possession* into different explanatory models.

The discomfort I feel when writing about *spirit possession* in the context of children's selves and experiences probably mirrors the western resistance to these kinds of possibilities. I also find the word *spirit* problematic, as it can evoke limited definitions and conditioned meanings, associated with religiosity and new-age discourse. There is a further concern about something much more commonsensical – how these ideas could be shared with frightened parents and children who need logical and grounded explanations about their experiences. Parents/carers want to locate their children's experiences of PANS/PANDAS in biomedical models, viewing them as psychological disorders and other dysfunctions in the child. This is not surprising as there are sparse options for parents that need reassurance that their children can be healed.

Epilepsy, Narcolepsy and Children's Unexplained Experiences

The World Health Organization (WHO) estimates that there are 50 million people worldwide who have epilepsy, making it one of the most common neurological conditions globally. Epilepsy is characterized by seizures which are caused by excessive electrical activity in the brain. The effects and impact of epilepsy vary depending on which part of the brain is affected. Studies on epilepsy suggest 30% of people with epilepsy experience behavioral and psychiatric problems.[131] Like children's unexplained experiences, persons with epilepsy are often studied in clinical contexts, from predefined ideas that claim their experiences are symptomatic of epilepsy. Louise M. King, a researcher at Northampton University in the UK, ran a qualitative research study with nine adults with epilepsy. The aim of King's study was to gather meanings about the living experiences of people with epilepsy, offering "a voice for an often ignored and stigmatized group."[132] King's findings show how people with epilepsy (included in her study) qualify their experiences as transpersonal. Their experiences share the qualities of phenomena such as mystical states, NDEs, OBEs and more. King identified themes that emerged from participants in the study. People described their experiences of seizures as moving through a portal to different realities, receiving a download of wisdom and engaging with other presences. Two participants reported mediumistic capabilities and most participants reported how their experiences shaped their sense of self. These experiences were transformative. King's results are very similar to findings from my own studies with children.

An article from 2006 details a study involving 221 university students who meditated, and 860 who did not meditate.[133] The author notes how student meditators displayed a wide range of complex, epileptic-like signs, such as experiences of vibration, hearing one's name called, religious phenomenology and a range of other types of unexplained experiences. How many years a participant had meditated were correlated with the incidence of phenomena, including sensed presences. Connections are made in the article between alterations in neuron behavior, meditation and unexplained experiences that are identified in people with epilepsy. An interesting case study was published in 2004 by parapsychologist Alejandro Parra, about the recurrent spontaneous psychokinesis (RSPK) experiences of 18-year-old Andres Vernier. The household had been experiencing strange happenings, poltergeist activity in the form of large stones thrown around the home and walls and furniture destroyed. Andres had frontal lobe epilepsy, experiencing blanks since age nine and seizures from 12 years, along with a range of other emotional issues. The poltergeist activity was intense and frequent, only stopping when Andres attended the hospital and had taken medication to sleep. After extensive tests and support from different experts, Andres' family concluded that he was a PK agent – creating the poltergeist activity with his mind. The author conjects a model that may explain the PK activity caused by Andres, as a displacement of his repressed aggression. The emotional energy and difficulties for Andres to communicate, creating a PK force.

Narcolepsy also affects brain functioning and can cause sleep paralysis and *hallucinations* in those with the condition. It is extremely rare for children to have narcolepsy and studies note that it is a condition that may be under-reported in children. One little boy I researched with was diagnosed with narcolepsy and cataplexy at the age of five years. Cai was six years old when he first shared his experiences with me.

> Cai: When I go toilet, I see people in the water don't like it it's scary like them spiders.
> R: Ah spiders? Do you want to tell me about them?
> P_02 (Cai): Erm... hmmm. When I'm in bed with my mum they come (.) hmmmm I don't like them.

Cai was diagnosed with narcolepsy at the age of five years and has reported a range of unexplained experiences (seeing apparitions of people, animals and precognition). Cai reported seeing spiders in different rooms in his home. Medical literature shows that seeing spiders is also common in people with epilepsy. Other children in the study, without epilepsy or narcolepsy, reported seeing spiders. Common experiences for people with narcolepsy are sleep paralysis and *hallucinations*, explained as the effects of a loss of hypocretin-producing cells in the posterior hypothalamus (a chemical imbalance in spinal fluid). The neuroscientific model does not advance an understanding of *hallucinations* and the experiential authority of people is never sought. In some cases, hallucination does not appear to be an adequate explanation.[134] The above example comes from an article I published in 2021, about the healing potential of children's unexplained experiences.[135] Even in frightening experiences, children report positive after-effects that seem to continue. For example, one young person reported a withdrawal from medication following a peak experience. For Cai, the presence of scary spiders and strange beings in his home prompted an affinity with the superhero Spider-man. His identification with a powerful superhero gave Cai confidence and feelings of empowerment.

Epigenetics and Children

Troubling the distinction between mind and matter are studies conducted in the field of epigenetics. Since the late nineties, Professor of Psychiatry and Neuroscience Rachel Yehuda has studied epigenetic mechanisms in the intergenerational transmission of stress effects, such as PTSD and nightmares – in other words the biology of post-traumatic stress disorder. Yehuda and colleagues have evidenced how parental trauma can cause genetic alterations in their children.[136] These studies show how biological alterations caused by trauma (especially PTSD – post-traumatic stress disorder) in Holocaust survivors were also found in their children and grandchildren – who had not been exposed to trauma or any psychiatric disorder. As discussed earlier with PANS/PANDAS children, here is a case of children who have not directly suffered intense trauma yet are experiencing traumatic symptoms and mental material (in the form of memories and nightmares). Yehuda found that children from Holocaust survivors had the same neuroendocrine or hormonal abnormalities that were found in Holocaust survivors. Findings from the many studies conducted on groups such as pregnant mothers who experienced the 9/11 bombings and their children, "yield a cogent understanding of how individual, cultural and societal experiences permeate our biology."[137] How we experience reality through our perceptual field influences, not only our own bodies, but those of our children and grandchildren. In a recent interview with Yehuda, the host suggested that Yehuda's research in some ways resonated with passages from the bible:[138]

The fathers ate sour grapes, and the children's teeth were set on edge.
Ezekiel

The ancient quote refers to children's misfortune to carry the burden of the ancestors, that Yehuda is evidencing through genetic studies, whether "fair or unfair, it's a fact". The biblical quote refers to the father, yet Yehuda's research is showing that it is the mother who may transmit trauma. When studying mothers caught up in the 9/11 tragic attacks, Yehuda learned how there was a trimester effect on cortisol levels in the babies, showing how some of the differences between maternal and paternal trauma and risk may be linked with the special in-utero changes to developmental programming. This potential evolutionary move can create greater stress levels in children and adults in environments that do not meet the full repertoire of responses (for example a stress response to starvation in a country that may not have this issue). What is striking about Yehuda's observations is the importance of others. Holocaust survivors who were known to not access support, got through because of the presence of another – how we behave towards each other can affect our molecular biology. Whatever matter *is* it appears to be directly affected by mental processes and our subjective perceptions and experiences. Yehuda's studies with trauma-experienced expectant mothers resonates with Stanislav Grof's insights about fetus experiences of stress or toxicity in utero. The idea that children inherit their grandparents' trauma responses (chemically and psychologically) takes us back to Carl Jung's observation about great-grandparents being the true progenitors of children's psychic contents, fused within a participation mystique.

The Mind-Body Problem

Children's experiences reported in this chapter raise questions about the relationship between mind and body. Children whose bodies are inflamed experience unexplained phenomena and drastic alterations to their usual person, showing important correlations between mind and matter. Children inherit mental processes that affect their biology, from grandparents and beyond, and states such as dissociation, epilepsy and narcolepsy can trigger unexplained experiences. The mind-body problem has been cited as one of the most difficult problems to solve in science and philosophy. Queries that gather around this problem include: are they two separate things? How are they synchronistic and where are they held? If they are made of the same stuff, which is primary (mind or body)? Despite the persistent mystery, the mainstream metaphysics of Cartesian Dualism (an aspect of physicalism) assumes that matter or the body is primary; and the mind/consciousness is an epiphenomenon of physical objects (such as the brain). Despite science advancing this notion in different ways, rendering physicalism as a worn-out model, this is not reflected in the lifeworlds of everyday people. Systems are geared to supporting and enacting this dominant way of thinking about human beings and our relationship to our environment. This can be seen in the biomedical model with the medicalization of natural human responses to inner and outer circumstances.

I have only so far met one child who experienced spontaneous healing of a medical condition, following an intense peak experience. This is an area that I have not yet fully explored with children. There is an abundance of research into the relationship between well-being and unexplained experiences in adults, that show significant and enduring positive effects. Studies that examine adult unexplained experiences report how adults have a similar or better psychological adjustment compared to the average population.[139] Physical healing experiences have also been reported in research studies. For example, Larry Dossey notes that healing is a neglected aspect of NDEs. In a 2014 paper, Dossey includes case examples of people spontaneously healing from the very diseases that caused them to die. One example is the case of Mellen-Thomas Benedict who had an NDE in 1982. Benedict was dying from an inoperable brain tumor. Benedict died for 90 minutes. Within three days he felt well and happy and was discharged from the hospice where he thought he would end his days. Three months later, Benedict returned to see his doctor to be tested again. A follow-up brain scan revealed the brain tumor had disappeared. Western biomedicine would "explain healing experiences as lucky coincidences even though similar stories have been reported over the millennia."[140] But the growing evidence of cases such as Benedict's are starting to challenge the biomedical model.

In health science, the placebo and nocebo effects show promise for advancing ideas to address the mind-body problem. Placebo and nocebo are used in drug trials to show the effectiveness of new drugs. These trials take different control groups, giving one group the drug and the other group a placebo. With some conditions such as epilepsy, Crohn's disease and Parkinson's disease, placebos work well showing improvements for patients. Nocebo works the other way, creating negative side effects. There is a paucity of research into placebo and nocebo effects despite the potential of this phenomena to inform deeper understandings about the mind-body problem. The ability of the mind to create side effects in nocebo drug trials, or relief from pain and healing in placebo trials, needs better explanations than those presented through the biomedical literature. As does the phenomenon of children having birthmarks that correspond with past lives, or people healing their bodies through the mind. In the next chapter, I explore children's unexplained experiences through the lens of post materialist science.

Chapter 10

Children's Unexplained Experiences and Post Materialist Science

The day science begins to study non-physical phenomena, it will make more progress in one decade than in all the previous centuries of its existence.

Nikola Tesla (1919)

I always have a strong feeling there's something more than what everyone else feels about the world, like it's not just science... it's not black and white, sometimes people just feel things that no one else does which like I can't really explain it. Just because someone else doesn't feel it, doesn't mean it's not a real thing.

Chloe, aged 17 years

Throughout the book, there has been a persistent issue emerging that impacts on children, their unexplained experiences and their ways of being. The issue is found with the dominant physicalist worldview, that powerfully influences how human beings, phenomena and realities are experienced. The dominant worldview globally disrupts cultural and social contexts and has local implications for individuals and communities. The science of physics that alleges reality is made from physical objects occupies a privileged place in academia (and beyond). It is a scientific narrative that states everything to be physical – all objects, entities and events – or at least identical or reduced to physical things. This includes the mind or consciousness (taken to include our sense of self and phenomenal experiences). Once the brain dies, so does consciousness and those aspects of it that are so familiar. In fact, "physical science has come to claim a particular kind of hegemony over other subjects in the second half of this century."[141] Most contemporary mainstream science and scholarship, to some degree, is answerable to physicalism.

It's clear that physicalism (in all its variations) cannot explain children's unexplained experiences or ways of being. Nor does physicalism advance an understanding of the nature of mind, matter or reality. As we have seen throughout the book, children's unexplained experiences are often decontextualized or treated as a separate phenomenon. There are other ways to think about and understand unexplained experiences of children that I have started to progress throughout the book. A new wave of scholarship is emerging and growing that considers what it means to be human and the nature of reality in exciting ways. Within the disciplines of philosophy, science, psychology, biology, physics and cosmology, scholars and scientists are breaking down old ways of thinking about the world and inviting others to consider these empirical, theoretical and philosophical possibilities. In this chapter, I focus on science, weaving children's experiences with different scientific accounts of the world proposed by scientists such as Bernard Carr, Donald Hoffman and Dean Radin. These scientists are offering a new vision of the world and our relationship to it.

Children in a Material World

In contemporary society, any facts about children's unexplained experiences are deduced from facts about a physical reality. In the domain of health science for example, children's unexplained experiences are explained as symptoms with biological causes. Modern physics works from the idea that there is a complete physical explanation for reality, except that consciousness is not part of this complete description. The mind and subjective experience, it is suggested, emerges from the brain and its activity, without adequate explanations of how this happens. We may find this to be plausible, when reflecting on children's unexplained experiences that may correspond with brain disorders, or the ways cognition is affected by drinking alcohol or banging one's head. These examples only serve to describe some type of correlation between brain and mind. There is no evidence to suggest that the mind emerges from the brain. Cognitive scientist, Donald Hoffman, explains this through a train analogy. If several people turn up to a train platform, then a train arrives five minutes later, did the train arrive because people were waiting?[142] The answer Hoffman gives is *no*. There is a third factor, the train timetable that caused people to arrive at the station five minutes before the train. Hoffman through this analogy is bringing critical attention to the idea of causality – the traditional idea that the brain causes consciousness because there is a correlation. It is not so clear cut. Despite the challenges towards physical science and the rise of different versions of materialism, modern society is organized on the principle that everything is physical, having huge implications for many children (adults, animals and the natural world).

Pure physicalist science is based on Newtonian physics, or laws of nature (gravity and motion), that render the universe to be mechanical, filled with inert matter. Newton's calculus meant the universe could be measured and quantified through a language of mathematics. Humans, as rational beings, could comprehend the entire universe. In this way, reality (and self and experience) is based on observable facts. For scientists who subscribe to the materialist narrative, reality is made up of things and experience only emerges when these physical things are arranged in complex ways. Some scientists believe that things themselves have no objective aspects to them, like color or taste. For example, the taste of the apple is not in the apple, rather the taste is in the brain, or at least complex arrangements of brain activity. This may seem counterintuitive, as human beings seem to experience others and the world as real, existing independently from each other. As philosopher Bernardo Kastrup points out "although many different worldviews vie for dominance today, the academically endorsed physicalist narrative defines the mainstream."[143] Especially in areas such as neuroscience, that studies the brain and consciousness.

Brain Science

Connections have been made throughout the book between unexplained experiences and brain function. For example, there may be some correlation between conditions that affect brain functioning and unexplained experiences of children, such as in epilepsy or PANS/PANDAS. If studies are showing how a reduction in brain activity leads to exceptional experiences, as in the case of psychedelic users and meditators, it follows suit that any condition that impairs brain activity would induce a broader spectrum of experience. This does not in any way suggest that the brain produces consciousness. Rather, it shows how the brain may have a more passive role than material neuroscience would have us believe. In mainstream neuroscience, the brain produces consciousness. If brain activity is impaired, and conscious experience becomes richer, this could not be the case.

There are different models for explaining the function of the brain. The productive model is the mainstream explanation of brain producing consciousness. Contemporary research that advances models of mainstream neuroscience, is found in studies by Stuart Hameroff and Sir Roger Penrose,[144] who propose a *microtubule* account of how consciousness is produced. The idea is that there are microtubules inside the skeleton that have quantum wave functions. If this was the case, brain functioning would be more complex, expanding the 10-20 billion neurons of our brains, into unlimited numbers. Our brains would have more *computational* power. Another way for thinking about the brain and consciousness is the transmissive model. William James began this model of brain function by suggesting consciousness being filtered through the brain, like when color is sifted through a prism.

Neuroscientist John Eccles[145] suggests a fundamental particle called a psychon, whose job is to interact with our brains and wider fields of consciousness. The idea of brains interacting with nonmaterial fields has been advanced by Neuroscientists such as Michael Persinger and Nicolas Rouleau. Stanley Koren and Michael Persinger[146] came up with the idea of *The God Helmet.* Persinger designed and experimented with a helmet that was placed over the temporal lobes of individuals. In darkened rooms, participants experienced a range of unexplained phenomena, initiated by magnetic fields acting on the temporal lobes. Certain configurations of magnetic fields would produce different types of experiences, such as OBEs and sensing the presence of another. The research shows how the temporal lobes are highly sensitive, corresponding with natural experiences such as epilepsy. The experiments altered how brains interact with whatever is outside (in this case electromagnetic fields). The brain is passive and alterations in its functioning allow for interaction with nonmaterial fields.

Neuroscientist Nicolas Rouleau suggests how our brains are connected to the electromagnetic fields of the Earth. The earth generates magnetic fields at 7.8 megahertz which overlaps with brain states known as beta and theta, in real time (known as the Schumman Resonance). Beta and theta states correspond with experiences described as mystical or those that experience a unifying principle (oneness).[147] What this suggests is how deeply interconnected humans are to their natural environment – as children demonstrate. Rouleau has carried out research on human brains of deceased individuals to examine whether brain tissue still acts as a filter for consciousness. Brains from deceased people were placed into jars with a special chemical that retains the architecture of the brain (i.e., cells, networks etc.) – without the brains functioning. Rouleau wanted to show how brain tissue acted as an antenna, exposing the tissue to different electrical stimuli. The experiments show how the tissue filters differently, depending on areas of the brain. In one area, the parahippocampal gyrus, theta wave frequencies were detected, resonating with geomagnetic fields of the sun. Advances in neuroscience like Rouleau's are showing how interconnected human bodies are with the natural world. Our histories and the cultural stories of our ancestors correspond with these ideas.

Filter theories and transmissive models propose mind and matter to be separate things but do suggest a field of consciousness that our brains filter rather than produce. Other ways for thinking about the brain propose a reducing valve function, rather than a filter. English writer, Aldous Huxley (1894-1963), saw the biological function of the brain as a reducing device, eliminating and inhibiting consciousness to sustain an adaptive self. The *cerebral reducing valve* proposed by Huxley naturally limits mental processing that is biologically useful.[148] The cerebral reducing valve emerges during childhood. Before it has developed, children have the capacity to live in a *visionary world* with experience becoming restricted into adulthood. What then is the brain *reducing*? For Huxley, it is consciousness or mind at large. If the brain is underactive or leaky, the mind allows too much mind-at-large to enter conscious awareness (Strawson, 2018), resulting in unexplained experiences. This model of the brain as a reducing valve, I believe, could explain children's experiences and ways of being in more logical ways.

Children and the Matrix of Information

Science in its mainstream form contradicts the living experiences of children shared throughout the book. Yet, we do *seem* to experience a world in which we are separate from other people. We *seem* to experience being inside a body, interacting with others and a world – and everything we engage with in the modern world (such as the media, education, social orders) sustains this idea. For some time, scholars in social science have recognized problems with the materialist model of reality for explaining human beings. Some social theorists, such as Karen Barad, appeal to Niels Bohr's quantum physics to challenge physicalist "facts" about being human. Barad's *Agentive Realism* theory[149] argues that matter has been forgotten in social science; instead, it is already figured into the linguistic and mental domains. Barad suggests the material and discursive (language, mind and social practice) are mutually implicated in a process called *intra-action*. This is a mutual partnership, with neither one being prior to the other and neither being reducible to the other. In this way, agents or selves are entangled, there are no individual agents, selves only arise through intra-action. Social science theories like Barad's, valuably, aim to dissolve duality between subjects and objects and culture and nature. What they don't seem to do is address the duality proposed between mind and matter. There is also a potential for matter to be privileged over mind, rendering social science with the same problem that new materialists aim to address.

Bringing the body back into social science has real benefits for researching with younger children, as infants demonstrate an embodied and non-local subjectivity, a natural "worlding of children that does not divide children and nature or nature and culture, but instead proposes mixed up worlds in which all manner of things co-exist."[150] If matter is privileged in new materialisms, we need to understand what it is. New materialism science appeals to Gilles Deleuze's philosophy of difference.[151] For new materialism, human beings are temporary assemblages of (positive) differences; when brought together momentarily, they create a whole. Beneath this assemblage is nothing, no unifying force or genesis, nor subject or experiencer. Human beings, animals and other living organisms are accidental results of positive differences, that dismiss the intuitive teleological bias (meaning and purpose of things) children are shown to demonstrate (see next chapter).

Like Karen Barad, professor of cognitive science, Donald

Hoffman, also appeals to a form of *agentive realism* to challenge mainstream science. For Hoffman, universal consciousness is primary and is a set of conscious agents, connected to each other through a nonphysical network. Hoffman suggests that particles are vibrations of interacting conscious agents (rather than waves as suggested in quantum physics), allowing scientists to reinterpret physical properties such as position, momentum and energy – as properties of interacting conscious agents. Human minds could emerge from the combination of many elementary conscious agents. Donald Hoffman has spent the last three decades studying perception, artificial intelligence, evolutionary game theory and the brain. Hoffman's work has led to an interesting hypothesis that states the world presented to us through our perceptions is nothing like reality. Evolution has masked the truth of reality, enabling human beings to survive and function in the world. The idea that humans shape reality through their perceptions, on a user interface, doesn't imply that the objective world resides in human brains. Rather, there is an objective reality out there: if not for our user interface (perceptions, cognition etc.) – we could not survive.

Hoffman makes clear that his hypothesis is rooted in science and is developing a mathematical model to account for his *conscious agents* theory. Other scientific models can reframe matter as information. According to physicist Claus Metzner, "objective reality could be a huge array of numbers, an abstract matrix that holds a momentary state of the universe."[152] This would account for the world feeling consistent and address that fact that we all share the same reality. Metzner explains how an individual's virtual reality is rendered from the information matrix. At the same time, the matrix is shaped by individual virtual reality. In the matrix model, matter is viewed as information that unfolds according to fundamental laws of nature. Scientific models that are starting to reframe the nature of matter could start to advance better explanations about children's unexplained experiences. Challenges to mainstream physicalism should have consequences for sciences that study the human mind and behaviors such as psychology or social science. Historically, these disciplines that deal with subjective experience have been molded from physicalist scientific values – as a means for gaining status as a *real* science or legitimate discipline. The problems derived from legitimating research with people from physicalist research (observation, empiricism, measurement) has been discussed in previous chapters.

Children's Unexplained Experiences in a Quantum World

Scholars of parapsychology are turning to quantum mechanics as a scientific model that could account for experiences such as ESP and psi, despite the subject having notoriety for being very difficult to understand. Classical ideas about the physical universe founded in Newtonian science have been challenged through Quantum Mechanics (QM). Newtonian classical mechanics states that space is distinct from the body and time passes in a uniform way – independent on anything or anyone in the world. The world in Newtonian science is material and space only an abstraction that we use to compare different arrangements of things that make up matter. Albert Einstein's "theory of relativity" challenged long-held Newtonian ideas by proposing different ideas of time and space. According to Einstein, space and time are intertwined in an infinite fabric, like a stretched tapestry. Einstein suggested that light is made up of individual pieces or particles and not waves. These particles were referred to as "Quanta" and began a movement towards quantum mechanics – studies of the universe at the smallest scale (electrons, particles, photons etc.). Quantum mechanics shows how matter is not physical at all but constituted by wave-particles that can behave in ways that challenge classical physics.

Where classical mechanics states that objects exist in a specific space at a specific time, quantum mechanics suggests that objects exist in a state of probability. One of the most surprising discoveries in modern physics is how objects are not as separate or as solid as they appear to be. The deeper matter is explored, the more entanglements between things are found. Albert Einstein referred to this as "spooky action at a distance", with entanglement being one of the core principles of quantum mechanics. An important finding in quantum studies is the role of the observer. When an observer is watching, particles can also behave as waves. When particles behave as waves, they can pass through several openings in a barrier then meet again on the other side. The strange thing is that this can only occur if no one is observing. When an observer starts to watch the particles move through the opening of the barrier, the images change dramatically (the particle goes through one opening). This means when particles are observed they are forced to behave like particles instead of waves. The observer has some effect over them.

Much has been written about how quantum mechanics could provide a framework for explaining the unexplained experiences of people, suggesting how they may result from interactions between mental and physical fields.[153] In his book *Entangled Minds*, scientist Dean Radin explains how the view that quantum entanglement has no effect in our everyday lives is changing. Radin recognizes how quantum theories are still in their infancy – but can provide new ways for thinking about psi experiences. No longer are psi experiences regarded as rare human talents, divine gifts or powers that magically transcend ordinary physical boundaries. Instead, psi becomes an unavoidable consequence of living in an interconnected, entangled reality.[154] From a quantum entanglement perspective, many types of children's unexplained experiences would appear normal or logical. Quantum entanglement is a phenomenon found within the smallest levels of the universe, at very tiny subatomic scales. It is a state that finds two or more objects that may be separated by vast distances still connected. One cannot be described without reference to the other. Scholars who study healing have used quantum entanglement to explain how the therapeutic interaction involves some type of interaction between people reconciling ideas of spooky action with living systems.[155] In my own studies, children have described a type of entanglement between thoughts, feelings and bodily sensations:

Image 11: I know my friend's thoughts, I feel my friend's pain

Emma tries to explain how she can be overwhelmed at times, as she feels her friend's bodily sensations, can hear her thoughts and experience her emotions. The drawing was an attempt by Emma to represent this entanglement in some way. Interestingly, the character in the middle of the two "stick people" (Emma and friend) is also Emma – her transpersonal self. The *intra-action* between Emma and her friend has given rise to the transpersonal self that Emma experiences, according to Emma's reflections. Children report experiences of acquiring information at a distance (time and space) through experiences traditionally thought of as extrasensory perception. Mainstream scientific thinking cannot accommodate children's unexplained experiences unless they are pressed into biomedical discourses and reframed as symptoms. In fact, the mainstream paradigm still cannot explain our simplest subjective experiences, that are usually dismissed as epiphenomena generated by the brain. The focus on unexplained experiences in children carries an urgency in the face of the increasing and sustained suffering of children and families in our current paradigm.

Children's Unexplained Experiences, Space and the Universe

Professor Bernard Carr is a renowned Cosmologist and Astrophysicist. Carr observes how mainstream physics doesn't seem to include the mind or our subjective living experiences, in their model of the universe. A new model of the universe is proposed by Carr to accommodate matter, mind and/or consciousness. The two dominant positions in physics, quantum (universe at the micro level) and relativity (universe at the macro level) need to be reconciled to achieve a Theory of Everything. While quantum physics offers a role for the observer, said to collapse the wave function, bringing the universe into existence – a deeper paradigm is needed to describe mental phenomena and our own living experiences. Carr posits matter as a derivative of consciousness and notes the possibility that the universe has extra dimensions. Carr's model proposes psycho-physical spaces that may account for paranormal or mystical human experiences.

I feel that Carr's model of the universe can offer a sound way to start to organize and think about unexplained experiences of children. I do this with caution, knowing that the complexity and intra-connected nature of human experience cannot be labelled and categorized. The aim is to take experience out of categories and start to think about them in terms of the spaces they may occupy – and how this may correspond with our very selves. Normally, unexplained experiences are categorized by experience type (for example Psi = telepathy, PK, precognition). These categories are not clear cut, as some experience types can bleed into others. What is exciting about Carr's model is that experience is understood in relation to space and states of consciousness. Carr distinguishes different mental states that involve "some form of communal space, which is not the same as physical space but subtly interacts with it." The universal structure that Carr proposes "can be regarded as a higher dimensional information space which reconciles all our different experiences of the world."[156] Children's play states may be a good example where there is an interplay and reconciliation of different psychic and physical spaces.

I've organized children's experiences identified across my own studies, within Carr's model of *Three Mental Spaces*. This exercise also shows the multilayered nature of subjective experience that can cut across these categories of space. I also include here how the "three senses of self" experienced by children and identified in chapter 7, correspond with Carr's Three Mental Spaces model:

1. Normal Space (Conceptual Self)

Phenomenological Space: Generated by perceptions of physical space through physical sensors
Children's Experiences: Names, bodies, ages, school, college, family, social media, homes, social places, health, mental health, contexts, intersections, shared social consensus (i.e. research, religion, culture, adult-responses)

Memory Space: Replay of images and events experienced through physical sensors in the past
Children's Experiences: Narrative accounts, trauma, holidays, relationships, growing-up, past life memories (unexplained experience that behaves as memory)

Visualization Space: *Generated and controlled by imagination, related to creativity*
Children's Experiences: *Methods, art, "play", sounds, metaphor and imagery*

Dream Space: *Like memory and visualization space but more vivid and with other elements*
Children's Experiences: *On the cusp of "paranormal space" – lucid dreams, dreams of other unfamiliar places (i.e. crystal cities) and shared dreams; younger children reported dreams and intuition as part of their "conceptual self", older children did not*

2. Paranormal Space (Transpersonal Self)

Psi Space: *Involves both mental and physical space so directly links matter and mind*
Children's Experiences: *Scopaesthesia (sense of being stared at), empathic abilities, telepathy, premonitions, telekinesis*

Apparition Space: *Different from physical space but with some aspects of externality*
Children's Experiences: *Engaging with deceased relatives, "imaginary friends", interacting or witnessing strange beings – tall faceless beings, strange animals, balls of light, shadow people, shape-shifting beings, UFO-sightings, friendly unseen beings; voice-hearing; sound-hearing; ADCs (After death communications)*

Threshold Space: *Pseudo-physical experiences on the threshold of sleep and waking*
Children's Experiences: *Sleep paralysis, engaging with other beings (relatives, strangers), travelling to other places (i.e., moving through the universe and planets)*

3. Transpersonal Space (Transpersonal Self)

OBE Space: *Resembles physical space but subtly different and changed by imagination*
Children's Experiences: *Out of body experiences, remote viewing*

NDE Space: *Relates to OBE space but other space-like experiences are involved*
Children's Experiences: *Experiences of void, tunnels, meeting loved ones or strangers, meeting figures such as Jesus or angels, frightening experiences*

Survival Space: *Where "souls" dwell after death or between incarnations*
Children's Experiences: *Mediumship tendencies, messages for living people, after-death communication, visiting survival spaces in dream space*

Knowing I (identified by children – see chapter 6)

Mystical Space: *Associated with various extrovertive experiences including higher planes*
Children's Experiences: *Peak experiences, bliss, oneness, gratitude, self-healing, dissolution of personhood/child status*

If children's selves and unexplained experiences were understood in mainstream society as corresponding to different mental spaces that model the universe, I propose that there would be a reduction of suffering (for children and adults) on a grand scale. Thinking about experiences such as premonitions as existing in a memory space, supports Ehrenwald's controversial view (see Chapter 3), that psi abilities are an extension of normal human perception – and Powell's later conclusions about savant children and telepathy. If there is a memory space, both past and future memories experienced through the physical senses may be accessible to children. Scientists have not located a part of the brain where memories are stored, with neuroscientists suggesting that memories may be non-local.[157] The paranormal space could account for children's spontaneous experience of *psychosis*, where they are bombarded with a range of visual, sound and smell perceptions that cannot be accounted for in the normal space. In the "Who am 'I'?" study (see chapter 6) spaces and selves did not seem separate for children. As a speculation made from observing children in self-enquiry research, shifts between selves or spaces could represent interactions between subtle layers of subjectivity, vibrating within a subject-at-large (knowing "I").

Experiences can cut across the porous boundaries of the mental spaces proposed by Carr.[158] For example, lucid dreaming could be placed in normal space, paranormal space, NDE space or transpersonal space. This corresponds with the senses of Self shown in the diagram in chapter 6, where children operate on multiple levels of self simultaneously, appealing to the idea that our "selves" may be multidimensional. This proposition is not so far removed from how *identity* is theorized in mainstream social theory. Sociologist Anthony Giddens suggested in the early nineties that our social identities are multiple and fluid. We shift into identities in accordance with social situations, roles and languages. For example, my multiple social identities include: an academic, a sister, a single-parent and so on. I sometimes occupy multiple identities, for example: a mother who must take her child to work must occupy the social spaces of academia and protective mother on campus. I'm sure as the reader you can resonate with this multifaceted way that we *be* and *become* in our social realities. So, the idea that our multidimensionality runs deeper is not so preposterous.

Post Materialist Science and Children's Unexplained Experiences

Science appears to be moving away from traditional ideas of a physical world with different models of matter emerging and scientists trying to explain how consciousness (subjective experiences and self) figures into it. The gap between progressive science, academia and social policy is still significantly wide. Some of the ideas that I have presented so far in the book would not be entitled to feed into research that develops health, education or children's policies. But what it may do, is inform parents, carers, professionals and other academics, to think about children and their unexplained experiences, in different and more logical ways. In my research practice, I can avoid situating children's unexplained experiences and ways of being in worn-out, mainstream materialist doctrines, and facilitate children to be with their own experience, in observational, critical and philosophical ways.

New ways of thinking scientifically about the nature of matter and the role of consciousness can start to inform a new model for situating children's unexplained experiences and the meanings they assign to them. Children's experiences and insights can contribute towards the continuing development of hypotheses, mathematical models and universal maps. A move away from physicalist science seems to suggest that mind and self is non-local and consciousness has a primary role in reality. Nature too features in rationalizing experiences that are viewed as unexplained. If the universe is entangled, a field of phenomena in which all minds and bodies are intra-connected, naturally, children's experiences would reflect this. More so, before the rigidity of sociocultural conditioning starts to limit how children experience self and reality. In the next chapter, I consider the philosophical ideas that can influence science and explain minds, bodies and consciousness, in ways that correspond with children's unexplained experiences and ways of being.

Chapter 11

Philosophy and Children's Unexplained Experiences

We are all brothers and sisters like loops of families... really we are all one big bubble.

Leo, aged 8 years

Some philosophers claim that young children cannot do philosophy... our beliefs that children cannot do philosophy are based on philosophical assumptions about children. My conclusion is that the very idea that very young children can do philosophy has not only significant consequences for how we should educate young children, but also for how adults should do philosophy.

Karin Murris (2003)

Children's unexplained experiences and ways of being can trigger philosophical questions, such as, *what is the world* or *why am I here?* Younger children are natural philosophers. This can be seen in their curiosities and relentless questioning about the world around them. Older children forget their need to question until an experience may remind them that there may be more to who they are. Childhood theorist, Karin Murris, notes how the debate on whether philosophy is suitable for children is an ancient one – a debate that is complicated by a confusion between doing philosophy as a subject (studying great thinkers) and philosophizing (asking questions in a philosophical way). There is a body of literature and organizations that promote children as philosophers in education.[159] Some of the criticisms of viewing children as philosophers suggest that children can perform "philosophical one-liners"[160] saying the same thing as a famous philosopher, only simpler. According to critics, adults will then project theories into the words of children – rather than it being a co-creation of philosophical ideas between children and adults. Criticisms of this type are often founded in certain ways for thinking about children and the study of philosophy, through reason, logic and abstract, complex thinking. These are ideas premised on set ideas about language, intelligence and reason, cognitive processes that children are not thought capable of performing. Young children may demonstrate abstract thinking through fantasy and play, using complex cognitive processes that are there prior to learning language.[161] Intelligence is often equated with language, where errors are made about children's capacities to use abstract thinking. Children in my own studies will use analogy and metaphor to describe reality and who they are, mixing the abstract with the concrete. Unexplained experiences, at times, cannot be grounded in the concrete by their very nature as being situated in space, content and time beyond the usual. Abstraction and logical reasoning in children manifest in ways different to traditional western conceptions of philosophy. As Gareth Matthews observes, adult philosophers would be better if they had more of the natural innocence of children.

The problem of language in philosophy is noted by Wittgenstein as "a struggle against the bewitchment of our intellect by means of language."162 The philosophical embodiment of younger children comes through acts of tasting mud, playing with worms and watching the concentric circles that form in puddles – before jumping into them. When children have experiences that betray a fixed self and reality, their questions become more complex, emerging from living experience that demands a deeper, abstract representation. Socrates observed how knowledge is there prior to learning, using the phrase I don't know in his own teachings, to privilege inner wisdom over technical learning. The philosopher Immanuel Kant also noted knowledge of time, space, causation and freedom was prior to experiencing the world.[163] Children's philosophizing is Socratic, as their many innocent questions lead to further enquiry.

Children and Reality

The exclusion of children from studies about unexplained experience are based on an idea that children are confused about a basic ontological distinction between reality and fantasy. Scholars from child psychology and education have explored how children make sense of what's *real* and what is *unreal*. Piaget in 1929 argued that children below the age of twelve years could not distinguish between reality and fantasy. Children, according to Piaget, are *artificialists* who misunderstood the limits of human creative power.[164] In a 2004 article, Deborah Kelemen argues that children are rather *intuitive theists* who are disposed to think of natural phenomena as resulting from nonhuman design. Meaning children logically believe the natural world to be a product of a nonhuman agent. Children's reasoning about living things, according to research, is constrained by teleological assumptions (reasoning about entities and events in terms of purpose) from a very early age. For example, children will explain parts of the body by reference to their self-serving functions, rather than their physical cause. This teleological bias (having purpose) for properties of both living and nonliving natural objects happens even when children are told that adults apply physical explanations to natural entities.[165] Research around this topic shows that children's intuitions around a grand designer of the natural world are not influenced by primary carers, religiosity or culture.

EM Evans conducted research in 2000 that found, regardless of the religiosity of their home-background, children show a bias towards intentional accounts of how species originate. Children from both fundamental and non-fundamental American homes favored creationist accounts about the natural world. Children from secular backgrounds in my own studies can theorize reality from an intuitive theism, as shown through Joe's picture here:

Image 12: A non-human agent holding the universe

Joe represents his view of reality as created and held by a nonhuman agentive being. Joe also suggested that all creatures (human, nonhuman including plant life) are all aspects of this agentive being. The being is neither male nor female but could be referred to as God (Joe is from a secular, nonreligious family and attends a nonreligious school). In fact, the only reason Joe has drawn a male god-type figure is because he did not know how else to represent reality. Joe is a little boy who demonstrates acute empathic abilities and has stated that the world "is not real" since the age of four years.

Kelemen *tentatively* suggests that children can be characterized as intuitive theists, which has relevance not only to cognitive theorists but also to science educators. The implication is that children's science failures may, in part, result from inherent conflicts between intuitive ideas and contemporary scientific thought. The philosopher Auguste Comte (1798-1857) described children and adolescents as being in a particular quest for meaning that cannot be found in science and religion – they are the ultimate philosophers. Scholars of child psychology often suggest that children confuse non-reality (such as fantasy, appearance and illusion) for reality.[166] These types of research studies are important for exposing how adults can influence children's reality status beliefs (such as Santa Claus and the tooth fairy), and to understand how children negotiate reality status. Child psychologists who study children's unexplained experiences (normally viewed as fantasies, night terrors etc.) suggest distinguishing reality from non-reality is one of the fundamental tasks of childhood.[167]

However, something very simple but extremely important appears to be absent from studies about children's sense-making regarding reality. The question *what do we mean by reality?* is never used as a starting point. Instead, scholars start from a preconceived idea, rooted in materialism, about what counts as reality and what counts as non-reality. In this way, unexplained experiences of children are assumed to be fantasy or imagined before considering adult beliefs about the nature of reality, that are often premised in physicalist models. Scholars argue that children rely on adult testimonies about reality as they cannot access metaphysical knowledge from traditional domains of history, religion and science – experiences that cannot be accessed directly. However, children (and adults) are shown to have direct experiences of states of consciousness that can be explained through metaphysical ideas.[168] These are often peak or transformational experiences that see people transcend the ordinary boundaries of personhood, space and time. Experiences that some claim catalyzed the world's religions.[169] Children access metaphysical knowledge through unexplained experiences that can cause either disruption or well-being, depending on how children are supported.

Through the "I"(s) of Children

There's no doubt that children's views about reality can be influenced by adults, computer games, movies and peers. What is less often explored is how children theorize the nature of reality through their own unexplained experiences. Children who experience phenomena such as lucid dreams, out of body experiences, near-death experiences and peak experiences often have a strong sense of a reality that contradicts mainstream views. In my roles as a researcher, as a mother and as a volunteer, I often hear the theories of children about the nature of reality. At the risk of putting "philosophical ideas into the words of children", there is a new body of scholarship that corresponds with children's ways of being, unexplained experiences and views about the nature of reality. I see this process of seeking philosophical explanations as a co-creative venture between children and the philosophical minds of our modern times. I attempt to weave through this section children's own philosophical views and unexplained experiences, with current models that explain the nature of self and reality. The philosophical turn sees new ideas emerging that position consciousness as having a fundamental reality, such as cosmopsychism, panpsychism and idealism. It goes beyond the scope of this book to explain the core tenets of each approach. I only include general descriptions of philosophical ideas that correspond with and explain children's unexplained experiences and ways of being. Hopefully, described in ways that are meaningful to readers who support or who are interested in children and their unexplained experiences.

Ideas about reality by older children often come through a direct experiencing of phenomena that is catalyzed through suffering, peak experiences or sudden traumatic events (like my own described at the start of the book):

I just felt this click, like the penny dropped and I just realized it was like, the tree is life... this is actually what life, is everything around you. I was everything, I didn't feel like I was an individual, I felt I'd lost my ego if you know what I mean (?) like my mask dropped and I was just me and it felt so normal and natural.

Callum, aged 14 years

Callum describes who he is (in the moments of his peak experience) as being everything. His sense of individuality was dissolved but he still retains a strong sense of I-ness. The individual self is seen through, referred to as a mask slipping off. The important feeling Callum emphasizes is *natural*. This sense of self was described as natural by several children who have reported these types of experiences. Any account of reality, self and unexplained experiences needs to include the simplest explanations and those closest to nature. For Callum, reality is a web of interconnected processes. His self, in relation to the web of reality, is the space that holds it. As Callum has progressed, he still retains these ideas of reality, knowing that his individuality is a mask (albeit an important one, needed to participate in the world).

Dougie reports an experience he had while camping in nature, and the after-effects of his experience when trying to integrate back into the world:

For months I could see that everything wasn't real... birds would be the most beautiful thing I ever saw... the floor wasn't solid, it was made of this like waves and kind of geometric patterns... it was so like blissful for a while... then I started to have all these weird experiences like hearing a voice call my name, having really powerful lucid dreams and things like that.

Dougie, aged 16 years

Dougie's sudden peak experience (that he refers to as "blissful") meant that his usual experience of the world, as a separate individual, was ruptured – with positive and negative implications. Dougie's experiences are very similar to my own. It seems that Dougie had a tangible, deep and felt experience of self/reality, that made it difficult to participate in the world. Anything that appeared stable and solid before, gave way to the world as ephemeral, nonmaterial and temporal. As Dougie began to integrate, he was assaulted by a range of unexplained experiences, almost as if caught in a liminal space between worlds. I know this state well, having been exposed to a self/reality that is *realer than real*. Children access contents of a collective consciousness that we do not usually access. Dougie describes the nature of reality as "a dream". Nine-year-old Aliya agrees with Dougie about the nature of reality as dreamlike, concluding this through her own experiences of lucid dreaming and travelling through the cosmos.

Bubbles bursting, things clicking and masks dropping are metaphors used by children to explain a shift in how they experience reality. This is often connected to a shift in how they experience their self. Self and reality become deeply intertwined for older children who have experiences noted as *ego-death* in the psychological literature. Dougie describes seeing material objects as fluid (like waves), noting geometrical patterns in the composition of the solid floor. Everything they have been told about reality, about who they are, is rapidly dismantled through these types of experiences.

Children and young people who have unexplained experiences challenge mainstream views of reality:

R: Researcher; YP: Young Person
Lucid Dreams, 2019

R: So, reading something that tells you it's not normal or is something like schizophrenia, how does that make you feel?
YP: Scared (.) worried but I just feel that there is nothing wrong with me (.) it's not just black and white what people say (.) I don't think you know that science can have all the answers or explain things.
R: OK.
YP: It's a bit like what happened when I heard that new song called

Lucid Dreams, *do you know it?*

R: No. I've not heard that one.

YP: There's this song that's come out called Lucid Dreams *so I looked up what it meant and thought hang on I always do that but again my friends don't and I thought it was just normal and was how everyone dreamt.*

R: Can you tell me what you mean by lucid dream? What happens when you dream?

YP: Yeah, I wake up in my dream and I can control my dream like change what happens in it and things.

R: That sounds really interesting, could we talk about that when we meet next?

YP: Yes (smiling).

Poppy's comments show how children are not always influenced by popular culture. In this case, Poppy researches the meaning of lucid dreams after hearing the lyrics of a song – then realizes that she has had this experience (that she considered normal). Poppy challenges mainstream science about her own experiences. Children's unexplained experiences, and consequently, their views about reality are in tension with the consensus. This can create tremendous difficulties for young people like Poppy, who stay true to their own experiences and worldviews.

> I don't know something isn't real about it, it is a like a computer game when you die you get respawned.
> Zane, aged 8 years

Zane's comment could be dismissed as inferential to a child who plays computer games. In this case, virtual reality provides a metaphor in which Zane can relate his own experientially shaped views about reality. Here, Zane is discussing the concept of reincarnation (Zane reported past life memories at a younger age). The process of "respawning" in video games is where the avatar "dies" and then returns to the game – a useful analogy for explaining reincarnation.

Older, rather than younger children, reflect more on the mind and consciousness:

R: Researcher; YP: Young Person
Dialogical Thinking, Aged 16 Years, 2019

> YP: I'm aware of a voice in my head and when I ask my friends they say they don't have it.
> R: Can you describe the voice you're aware of. Is it different to your own?
> YP: It's not different but it's not mine... I mean it's not like hearing a different voice but these voices have opinions about things and can argue.
> R: Ah... could these voices be more like thoughts?
> YP: Yes they are but they don't feel like mine or me and then I heard no one has this so like when I ask my friends they say I don't have a voice in my head and then on social media other people say they don't.

Some children and young people are very aware of their thought processes, as shown in the example above. Even identifying higher-order dialogical thought processes that occur when we are problem-solving (for example). Young people are quickly labelled at times, even by their own peers who may not be as "conscious" of their thoughts. This meta conscious activity enables younger children and older children to observe their inner worlds. Children have identified different senses of self through this process:

R: Researcher; C: Child
Two "Me's", Aged 10 Years, 2019

R: *What does the word "I" mean to you......?*
C: *(silence – P_06 tends to fall into a silence before answering questions) I don't know (.) it's like there are two of me. This one here (moves hands to the left) and this one is where I want to dress and be the way I do.*
R: *That's really interesting (.) is that something we could explore more?*
P_06 *(C): Yes (smiling).*

It's almost as if I'm watching something on TV but like what I'm watching is me.
Kasey, aged 17 years

Aaron was 10 years old when I researched with him (see example above). What struck me about Aaron was how he would take long silent pauses before answering any questions. Silence is not often attended to in social research but has well-established roots in philosophy, found in ancient mysticism as "the ineffable, the inexpressible whereof one cannot speak, thereof one must be silent."[170] Silence seemed to be an epistemic bridge for children as they appear to generate knowledge from different senses of self. Aaron embodied his explanation of self by referring to spaces outside his body (moving hands), while identifying a self that gets dressed and acts in the world (hands move towards his body). Kasey had a transformational experience in hospital following a suicide attempt. Kasey describes becoming overwhelmed by a deep sense of gratitude that "flipped a switch" in how she felt herself and the world to be. In the quote above, Kasey uses a TV metaphor to explain how she senses two different senses of self; one that is an experience (Kasey) and one that observes the experience. Kasey alludes to a reality that is a screen of perception, where her "little me" appears. Children's experiences and views about self and reality raise questions about the nature of consciousness. So here, I turn to consider how modern philosophers are theorizing self, experience and reality, identifying which could better account for children's unexplained experiences.

Defining Consciousness

Entering the domain of philosophy is difficult for a social researcher. When I first arrived at philosophy, it was to try to get some understanding of my own experiences, then children's. The *hard problem of consciousness* was discussed everywhere, and the definition of consciousness not really discussed enough. The first trouble I had was trying to work out the word *consciousness*. Its usage is so variable, having different meanings dependent upon who is using the word, that it can lead to huge misunderstandings between scholars. The same issue can be seen with the term *self*, used in very different ways in social science, normally to refer to a narrative self or personhood. Philosopher Max Velmans also recognizes a problem with language in consciousness studies and proposes simple principles for defining consciousness. Once a definition of consciousness is firmly grounded in its phenomenology, according to Velmans, "investigations of its ontology and its relationship to entities, events and processes that are not conscious can begin."[171] Velmans advocates for a philosophy known as reflexive monism. In this view, there are two ontological categories (basis for reality) that are mental and material. Velmans suggests they are held in a reflexive relationship in a conscious universe. It is odd, according to Velmans, that we have no agreed definition of consciousness, especially as we have psychological data about what it is like to be conscious – and this is a result of theories of the "universe intruding into definitions of consciousness."[172] The frustration with semantics (words and meanings) can be attributed further to how scholars think about consciousness. Complexity theorists define consciousness as a property of the brain, emerging from complicated activity. Reductionists claim consciousness to be nothing more than a function of the brain. These ideas inform mainstream psychology, reducing consciousness to some aspect of human information processing.

Consciousness supersedes usual discursive (language) problems – it is not only a semantic problem. With that said, the worlds of science, philosophy, academia and the everyday would benefit from some consensual agreements around its meanings. The simplest place to start would be to see consciousness as that which we experience. Some scholars will make a distinction between being conscious and being non-conscious when in states, for example, such as dreamless sleep. Yet children can report experiencing deep sleep, in similar ways to the children who felt a "knowing I". Recent studies in cognitive science suggest that the assumption consciousness disappears in deep sleep is oversimplified, noting good empirical and theoretical reasons for saying a range of sleep experiences distinct from dreaming exist. Studies on dreamless sleep experiences are receiving growing attention.[173] Dreamless sleep cannot be accurately described as a uniform state of consciousness; instead sleep supports a range of different types of experience that are distinct from dreaming and occur outside rapid eye movement (REM). We may not be aware of all that we experience, as discussed through examples by children in earlier chapters.

A Living Experience Philosophy

As the aim here is to stay close to the experiences of children, any model of reality must prioritize living experiences. Political philosopher, Hannah Arendt, once suggested that theorizing can only arise "out of incidents of living experience and must remain bound to them as the only guidepost by which to take its bearings."[174] Arendt's concept of experiential authority originates in ideas about children's *natality* – or knowledge about being in the world that is there prior to learning. *Natality*, according to Arendt, should be something to be protected at all costs from the status quo that is pushed in education. Knowledge for Arendt is a blending of living and everyday experience with philosophy. Philosopher Miri Albahari links the lived experience of mystics with a proposed way of thinking about the world, through a model of "perennial philosophy."[175]

Like other scholars in the field of philosophy, Albahari notes a discontent with the dominant explanations of reality and their propensity to *paper-crack* – or mask critical problems in their ideas. For example, materialism has the hard problem of consciousness,[176] the inability to explain how simple subjective experiences arise from brains. Or the popular panpsychism theories that suggest smaller subjects or consciousnesses are found in the smallest materials (such as atoms, particles). Together, conscious atoms and particles somehow create a large subject (people). Cosmopsychism is a philosophy that proposes one universal consciousness that contains many smaller subjects. Papering the cosmopsychism crack, for Albahari, is trying to explain how one subject becomes many (decomposition problem). Albahari turns to the ancient mystics and reports of accessing an "aperspectival witness consciousness", that mystics define as reality itself. Albahari valuably appeals to lived experience to account for consciousness as the ground of reality that can be accessed through our everyday selves, as "if such unconditioned consciousness is what it purports to be (from the many reports of mystics), then it will not, as many suppose, be utterly divorced from our everyday conscious states."[177] Not everyone agrees with Albahari's statements about the value of lived experience. For example, philosopher Daniel Dennett denies the existence of phenomenal consciousness (feelings, sensations, perceptions etc.). His explanations of reality ride roughshod over phenomenal experiences, as he postulates how first-person living experiences can tell us nothing at all about reality. Only third-person, objective observations can do that.

There are many problems with statements like Daniel Dennett's, the most obvious being his own subjective dismissal of the existence of phenomenal consciousness. Another is his attitude that can explicitly reflect the dominant systems of thought in mainstream psychology and other branches of science that work with people.

We do not need to go back in time and appeal to the mystics for lived experience as evidence of an aperspectival witness consciousness; we can also turn to children. There is a body of research on transformational experiences in adults, studies on meditators, research with psychedelics and people who have near-death experiences, where everyday people report the same experiences as the mystics. Children in my own studies have described an aperspectival witness state of consciousness, through naturally occurring experiences and self-enquiry research. They also describe this state as "the real me", "the natural me" and "I just know this is me". For children, this aperspectival witness consciousness has an element of subjectivity, demonstrated by the sense of I-ness or Me-ness that is still there when the conceptual self is not. This sense of self/subjectivity may not be as complex as that experienced from the perspective of a conceptual self, nevertheless, its inherent feature is a natural I-ness.

As the aim here is to find a view of reality that can account for children's unexplained experiences and ways of being, we need to explore what's on the table. A model of reality that is capable, of not just explaining abstract ideas, but one that could meaningfully inform how we shape social life and exist in the world. That's a tall order, but I believe people are ready to accept and embody new ways of being, experiencing and expressing who we are in the world. In this way, a philosophy is needed that is simple in its formulation, without the layers of complexity often seen when scholars attempt to reconcile difference. One that can logically dismantle the dominant materialist paradigm, while still having the ability to retain what is valuable. A good place to start is by exploring some of the philosophical options that are emerging in resistance to materialist systems of thought.

Pans, Particles and People

Panpsychism is a popular philosophy that explains consciousness as an emergent property of atomic particles and other small entities. Panpsychists propose that these small conscious entities, through complex systems, make up our larger self or subject. Panpsychism advances materialism by spreading mind through the body, with some scholars suggesting it could be a favored solution to the hard problem of consciousness[178] and an answer for biology and the psychological sciences.[179] Even with the more sophisticated advocates of panpsychism, consciousness is still viewed as a basic feature of matter. Panpsychists focus on the mind-body problem, the "challenge of understanding how the conscious mind relates to the physical world."[180] The aim is to account for consciousness and bridge a gap between the mental and the physical. Panpsychism affords a way for scientists to stay within the parameters of mainstream materialism, while positioning consciousness with a fundamental existence in nature – found in the basic building blocks of physical reality. Panpsychism could offer limited interpretations for children's unexplained experiences but its reliance on materialism weakens its explanatory power.

The first trouble a panpsychist will need to address is how simple fundamental consciousness could arrange itself into larger living subjects (such as a human being, a dolphin etc.). This is known as the subject-combination problem and scholars have no real answers. Some scholars suggest that self or subjectivity is the issue, creating the problems that arise in panpsychism and cosmopsychism. If there is no self, then we would not need to explain how many subjects form to make one, or how one subject could split into many. According to philosopher Annaka Harris, there are two types of self – one autobiographical and the other, a self that "amnesiacs refer to when they say I don't know who I am... a deeper sense of self, of being a single independent existing entity that has a precise center and location."[181] An illusion. Thinking back to children's experiences of self, Harris' observations of the autobiographical self correspond with children's own experiences of a conceptual and transpersonal self. Where we might depart from Harris is with how a deeper sense of self is defined and used to disclaim the existence of subjectivity – as the fundamental nature of reality. When children enter a deeper sense of self, it is not the same as amnesiacs who say, "I don't know who I am." Children do "know" and experience the "knowing I" that has no locality or center – only children struggle to conceptualize this knowing through language. Do amnesiacs, despite losing their autobiographical self, not still retain a sense of I-ness? The self that is just beyond the autobiographical self is experienced by children as collective or shared (the transpersonal self), rather than individual. I-ness seems to be a knowing element of objectiveless experience and object experience. If we equate subjectivity with an illusory self, this will inevitably lead to conclusions that there is no self. But there is still, according to living experience, a simple experiencer that remains, when the illusory self is seen through.

I don't think there is anything wrong with me, I just thought maybe *there is something else to me*.
Poppy, aged 17 years

Neuroscientist Anil Seth may argue that this stable sense of subjectivity or I-ness, that we believe is retained across the life course, may be a hallucination, a product of a brain that is a mechanical-prediction machine. Seth explains how people experience brain-change blindness with respect to the self, not recognizing that the self changes all the time, fostering "the false intuition that the self is an immutable entity, rather than a bundle of perceptions."[182] Seth makes a valuable contribution in scientifically asserting that our conceptual selves are an illusion, advancing the argument for self being far more than we currently believe. The sense of continuity described by Seth is different from the enduring self or I-ness that children experience beyond their conceptual self – often described by older children as self that has been reclaimed from early childhood. Usually, the experience of continuity described by Seth is a result of narrative thought and speech. Narratives provide a sense of continuity and chronological time and are experientially different from the timelessness ascribed to the I-ness defined by children, mystics and others. The self that is described by scholars such as Seth or Harris is identified by children as an experience itself. As Wozniak observes, "what is usually investigated as the phenomenal I can be interpreted as *object* rather than the *subject* of experience."[183] Any experience requires an "experiencer" but a legitimate concern (raised by Harris and others) is whether a pure subject (consciousness) is a subject at all if it has no perspective. Shani & Keppler address this concern to suggest that, in the absence of perspective, there remains:

> Ipseity or selfhood... a conscious presence devoid of form and objects, yet ready to assume ordinary qualitative tones and to serve as the apprehending recipient of objects if the right conditions for the emergence of an individual conscious perspective materialize.
> Shani & Keppler (2018)

A fundamental subjectivity is the primordial self of babies, the I-ness of children and the aperspectival consciousness of the ancient mystics. Not a self-reflective or human version of a subject. We tend to mix up ideas of subjectivity with story-making, intentional actions and more. We do not need to eradicate all ideas of subjectivity or science to account for the primacy of consciousness. We only need to turn to the experiences of people and a more powerful, explanatory account of reality.

Universal Consciousness and People

Reality, according to scholars of cosmopsychism such as Freya Matthews and Itay Shani, is cosmic consciousness, a field of simple subjectivity. Cosmopsychism is a model of reality that proposes "that the experiences of ordinary subjects are ultimately grounded in an all-pervading cosmic consciousness."[184] The *cracks* in cosmopsychism beg the question: how do individual, ordinary subjects emerge from one subject (cosmic consciousness) as the ultimate reality? Scholars of cosmopsychism propose different theories about how one subject could form into many. For example, Shani & Keppler appeal to a branch of physics known as electrodynamics, using interactions of electrical currents and magnetic fields, to explain the problem. Shani conceives of the ordinary self as a vortex, swirling from an oceanic background, "a cohesive system with a characteristic organization, or form, maintained through dynamic balance between opposing forces and tendencies."[185] Many mystics and philosophers have used similar water analogies to describe consciousness and its many forms. Water is liquid and flows, can turn to ice that becomes solid and evaporate to become steam, each form made from water.

For Shani & Keppler, cosmic consciousness has a limited state of subjectivity, described as a pure subject that does not have individual perspectives. When individual subjects form, they are conditioned through different forces, a little like the other factors needed to turn water into steam (heat) or ice (cold). This is similar with how our beliefs about the world are conditioned through language, stories and circumstances that shape our individual selves, shown earlier through children's experiences of self. For the purposes of staying close to children's living experiences, an explanation of decomposition would appeal to what is already observable and natural (i.e. "it feels natural", "it's the real me"). Which other processes in nature could show us how different subjects emerge from one? Scientist and philosopher Bernardo Kastrup offers an explanation, in a way that appeals to nature, human experience and empirical evidence.

Analytical Idealism and Children

In 2019, Bernardo Kastrup published *The Idea of the World*, a fierce and highly intellectual account of reality that presents a very real challenge to the mainstream physicalist paradigm. Kastrup dismantles the physicalist worldview, identifying its assumptions and offering a simpler and rigorous explanation of reality. It is a philosophical model that sees consciousness or *mind at large* as primary. Physicalism, according to Kastrup, is a model for explaining the world/universe and not a given truth. Mainstream science presents assumptions as facts, that are explanations about relations between things, rather than a fact about the thing itself. Mainstream science bases its facts on correlations between experience and brain activity, the fact that we all share the same world and how the world unfolds independently from our own desires, according to Kastrup. Anything that we experience is only ever through images and sensations. As Kastrup observes, "what we call the world is available to us solely as 'images' – defined here broadly, so to include any sensory modality – on the screen of perception, which itself is mental."[186] Similar observations were made by children in my own studies, seen in examples such as Kasey's description of how she perceives her "self" as on TV or the art produced by children in earlier chapters.

It is easy for some to assume that Kastrup's idea of the world implies that the world only exists in our individual minds (this is known as "solipsism"). This is not the case. Kastrup argues how the world is made up of an external reality that we are *seemingly* independent from. Physicalism would propose the external world to be made up of physical objects while analytical idealism would see the objective world as made from mind/consciousness. Just as our brains are the extrinsic appearance of our inner life (how brains look from a third-person perspective/an observer), the external world is the extrinsic appearance of a mind at large, from our third-person perspectives. This explains how we seem to share the same world. On the level of the social, the same world may be attributed different meanings, depending on the social and cultural influences that affect concepts and beliefs. What is striking about an analytical idealism philosophy is that it can still account for explanations about the world (through science for example). It is only the starting point that has changed, yet it is a simple change that could transform the world.

We know the world through experience, whether mundane, unexplained or exceptional. According to Kastrup, experiences are patterns of *self-excitations of consciousness*. Consciousness naturally excites in the same way that fundamental particles are self-excitations of a quantum field. Observations of natural self-excitation are found in areas of physics such as superstring theory and M-theory. A way to think about how consciousness self-excites is to picture a dancer. Different choreographies of dance will correspond with particular self-excitations of the dancer – the dance is not distinct from the dancer in motion.[187] Similar to Shani & Keppler, Kastrup proposes consciousness (also referred to as *mind-at-large*) as a pool of nature that is subjectivity itself. The I-ness of consciousness forms many subjects, serving as "the dative of experience, namely, as to that to whom things are given or disclosed."[188] This implies that the experiencer is the field of consciousness rather than the *seemingly* individual subject, corresponding again with children's observations of a separate self, that is an experience (rather than an entity experiencing). I-ness can be located in living experience beyond concepts, sensations and perceptions. The I-ness is described by children as *natural*, appealing to processes that can already be observed in nature. Kastrup refers to a natural phenomenon of *dissociation*, to describe how one subject forms into many. As discussed in earlier chapters, dissociation is a common phenomenon in children, especially teenagers – often defined as a dissociation from one's "whole self" that is synonymized with *personal identity*. Dissociation in children is viewed by clinical professionals as a coping mechanism to separate from "self" (personal identity). From another perspective, dissociation in children, could be an act of moving towards self, rather than away from it. Entailing a temporary disruption to their location in the world.

Kastrup appeals to a more severe form of dissociation referred to as dissociative identity disorder (DID) to explain how many subjects can form from one. In nature, human psyches are formed through cognitive associations such as thoughts and feelings (excitations). When a human psyche dissociates, cognitive associations are disrupted and new centers of self-awareness can emerge, referred to as *alters*. There is a wealth of empirical evidence in psychiatry to account for this process, with some studies showing how alters can affect the physiology of bodies. Consciousness, according to Kastrup, behaves in the same way, forming new localizations of self-awareness (people, animals). It is this type of dissociation that Kastrup uses to explain how consciousness divides itself into multiple centers of awareness. In this way, human beings, animals and other living entities are "alters" of a universal mind at large. Each alter, according to Kastrup, is a private qualitative field with porous boundaries. From an Analytical Idealism perspective, children are "alters" of a universal mind at large.

Child as Alter and Unexplained Experiences

Let us imagine for a second, how children's unexplained experiences shared throughout the book could be explained, if we consider children to be alters of universal consciousness. The proposition of child as alter would have to account for:

- Children's "mundane" subjective experiences and individual agency
- Children's unexplained experiences that suggest mind is non-local (telepathy, premonitions, OBEs etc.)
- How the mind can affect matter (birthmarks, medical conditions, brains)
- How children have memories of past lives and/or access knowledge that is usually inaccessible
- Children's experiences of self and ways of being
- Why children might be more inclined to have unexplained experiences than adults
- A naturalistic description of children's unexplained experiences and ways of being

It's important that any view of the world can account for all human experience. As discussed in earlier chapters, the simplest subjective experiences we have, are often overlooked. The mundane, subjective experiences of the personal self are as equally mysterious as those we consider unexplained, from the perspective of what things are. When children develop a separate sense of self, even if this is an illusion, it is an important naturally occurring process. Our personal selves offer a beautiful and dangerous experience of separation and individuality. Our narratives create a sense of duality, our stories aspiring us towards connectedness through the sharing of experiences, collective realities and meaningful agreements. Boundaries are important for children who are vulnerable (in some ways) in the world. Agency for children may be the *conscious probe* of a mind-at-large, experiencing reality from a third-person perspective. Decisions made about children's selves, bodies and lives are usually made by professional adults, enacted through well-intentioned parents and carers. The challenge therefore is to reconcile the illusion of an individual agential self with its importance for being in the world. Analytical idealism affords such reconciliation, acknowledging the conceptual or personal self as a private qualitative field while recognizing the vastness of its subjectivity. When children recognize this, they can reauthor the limited and conditioned stories that bind and constrain them.

As a solid, individual entity, as proposed by the physicalist worldview, it is impossible for a child to have experiences such as OBEs, NDEs, premonitions, shared dreams, visions and more. But children do have these experiences and as an *alter of mind at large*, these experiences become logical, modelled from the very processes, shown to us by nature – as in the case of DID (in all its forms i.e. *possession*, voice-hearing, teen dissociation etc.). For a child, boundaries of their qualitative field may be more permeable than the boundaries of adults, especially when adults may experience more *qualitative tones* than children. This being the case, it would be logical for children to access larger fields (such as the collective consciousness, experiences such as shared dreams or premonitions).

Clearly there is significant evidence for the presence of causally-effective mental activity that we cannot access through introspection... that could still be conscious, in the sense of phenomenally experienced somewhere in the psyche.
Bernardo Kastrup (2017, 560)

If an alter is a private qualitative field, it seems reasonable to assume that there are larger qualitative fields (i.e., such as the collective consciousness) with porous boundaries. Staying with the idea that a child's development is a process of boundary formation, it is likely (as Jung suggests – see chapter 8) that children access the contents of larger qualitative fields, prior to boundaries forming into later years. This may explain experiences such as intrusive, repetitive mind patterns, past life memories and intuitive knowledge. As discussed in earlier chapters, babies experience the world as one, their excitations ensuring they cry for food and locate their mother's breast. An infant's development is often mistaken for a progressive move towards a whole, integrated self, as the child resists and tries to hold on to her rightful position as omnipotent and omnipresent. She already existed before dissociation began. When child alters play, they pause dissociation as they enter the liminal between *inner* and *outer* worlds. Natural tones of creativity emerge, manifesting new worlds that as adults we can no longer participate in. This mirrors the teenage world of cyberspace, that subtly pulls teen alters from physical space-time, where they can experience different realities from their own avatar probes. As children show us when they report their dreams. Fields could be synonymous with the spaces described by Bernard Carr, with unexplained experiences, corresponding with particular senses of self or degrees of alter dissolution.

Kastrup suggests that our bodies (including the brain) are an appearance in nature. Matter is what our inner life looks like from the perspective of another alter (a third-person perspective). The outside world is the appearance (from a third-person perspective) of the inner life of universal consciousness or mind at large. This idea of the world implies there is no problem for mind and matter – they are different configurations of excitations of universal consciousness. Like the water analogy I used earlier. This idea of the world can also explain the habits of nature (how we all share the same world). If the brain is an extrinsic appearance of a child's boundary, then a correlation between mental experiences and the brain is expected. When the brain is compromised, such as in cases of inflammation, the boundary is disrupted and open to contents of a larger collective, dissociative field. A dissolution of the brain boundary at death, say, would expose children to exceptionally *real* qualitative phenomena.

Nature unfolds spontaneously according to laws or habits in a predictable and stable way. Nature naturally dissociates, not through a self-reflective act, but intuitively. Naturalism from a physicalist perspective would suggest that any experience that cannot be explained by physicalism is therefore supernatural. Children's unexplained experiences exist and arise in spontaneous ways (rather than induced by activities that can initiate similar experiences such as psychedelics, meditation techniques etc.). The I-ness experienced by children is reported as *natural* and *real*, their relationship with nature authentic and simple. Children's observations of their dream-states betray the nature of the world as dreamlike and their *intuitive theism* reminds adults that there are greater depths to what we may perceive from our conditioned perspectives. The important question is, *So what?* What difference does it make just to turn reality on its head and start from consciousness rather than matter? Well, it makes all the difference and could have valuable implications for social transformation. I explore this by "Tying the Threads" in the summary of the book.

Tying the Threads

It's important to bring those boots back on the ground following an excursion into the domains of science and philosophy, to think about the implications for children and wider social transformation. The research from my own studies, presented throughout the book, does not involve samples of thousands of children, reams of statistical data or any *proof* that children have *real* unexplained experiences. If the reader is seeking that, the point may have been missed. I believe that when children report unexplained experiences, they carry a reality in terms of what is true for them, measured through the meanings children assign to them – and how unexplained experiences affect the lives of children (and adults). More than that, narratives of experience are qualitative data. When reports of a phenomenon are persistent across qualitative data sets, we can strongly assume that there is something afoot. In this case, a strong prevalence of unexplained experiences across younger, and more frequently, older children (including teens). If we then bring discursive analysis into the mix, the data around how experiences are reported by children weigh heavily for the case of legitimacy. The language strategies children employ to *disclose* unexplained experiences include nominalizations (claims to truth), legitimating strategies (bringing other witnesses into the narrative) and emotional lexis (conveying their feelings around the experience). All these examples of linguistic features of unexplained reporting tend to point towards authenticity rather than artificialism.

Reauthoring children's unexplained experiences has involved an expedition into social and scientific realms – to texture, loop together – a tapestry of thought and living experience. The tapestry has pulled on many threads to rewrite a story of children's unexplained experiences in a post materialist world.

The main authors are children themselves. Those young beings, who through their own experiences and resistances to modern grand narratives can remind adults about the magic and mystery of being human. Are we prepared to listen? There is a real urgency now to return to exploring unexplained experiences with children. Each day, a child is diagnosed or silenced, taken from their families or perhaps ridiculed by others for their own living experiences. All because we have it very wrong. Our current mainstream view of the world is creating suffering for children, adults, animals and the planet on a grand scale. Children, naturally aligned with a subjective force, a collective transpersonal field and other spaces of reality, could guide us back to forgotten ways of being. If, as adults we are courageous enough to admit that we do not know and are prepared to step back into the unknown with children.

Systems are breaking down on a mass scale, worn out and no longer purposeful for humanity. Meaning has been lost, buried beneath the need to know more, to have more, to be more. Children's natural ways of being are reflected through their unexplained experiences. Whether in dreams, through play or jumping in puddles, children are already where they should be, while adults are left behind. We have forgotten how to play or be in eternity with an earthworm. We can't remember how to create different worlds, filled with exciting creatures, heroines and arch enemies. We don't hear the whispers of the ancestors telling us to slow down, be quiet and go sit with a tree. Children are not afraid to ask the big questions about reality; let's be inspired, follow suit and start to question everything we thought we knew about the world and the universe. I asked at the start of the book whether it is dangerous to study children's unexplained experiences. I conclude by stating that it is a necessity – not only for children's well-being but as a significant contribution to the growing post materialist scholarship. The need to remember our human potential has never been greater.

Being human is a contradictory affair. On the one hand, the complexity of being human requires selecting certain interdisciplinary threads to try to account for experiences, circumstances and happenings. Fundamentally, the nature of being human is very simple. As humans, we believe that anything important must be explained in complex ways – as I have attempted to do through the book – to justify children's experiences and my own observations, interpretations and conclusions. It's time to stop weaving, tie the threads together and present children and unexplained experiences in a post materialist world.

Children in a Post Materialist World

The primary trouble is the mainstream physicalist story that pervades and constructs our very selves and lives, in ways that separate and disempower children and adults. The book has focused on *children* but this is an intergenerational affair. Adults face more difficulties in reconnecting to a primordial self, constrained and constricted by the layers of conditioning, that began when we were children (and before). Adulthood implies that we're all grown up, responsible and in the know. Children are encouraged to attain an adult status and function in a very dysfunctional society. Let us as adults cut ourselves some slack and recognize that we don't really know. But not too much slack, as we still have a responsibility to look to our own conditioned patterns and belief systems – and be brave enough to question them – if we are to facilitate the birth of our next generation into a post materialist world. What would children's unexplained experiences look like in a post materialist world? This requires some imagination now, to envision what a post materialist world might involve. If consciousness is primary and our very being is shared, would we be so quick to separate and *other* our fellow alters – whether human beings, animals or the natural world? To know the nature of mind, in its connectedness with other minds and a larger field, would we be more attentive to the thoughts in our own and shared field – dropping *personal* responsibilities and focusing on changing what is stale and stuck? And what of our children? Would spaces and mentorship be available for young alters, their conscious probing informing and reminding their elders of their origins?

The social world may start to look different too. Modern social systems are modelled to create dependency on experts who know us better than we know our selves. But hang on – if in our post materialist ways, we prioritize knowing our*selves*, then surely, we no longer need institutional experts to tell us what to do with our minds, bodies and lives. As new systems of thought emerge through the sciences and philosophy, that reconfigure the nature of children, experiences and reality, systems of education may need to adapt. Opening their tight curriculums to include lost knowledge, modelling pedagogic practices in ways conducive to the post materialist child. Allowing children to learn in creative and liberating ways. Literacy would include image, art and symbol as ways to express the unlimited and unbounded selves and experiences of children. Nothing needs to be thrown away, mechanical science still leads the way in explaining how things may go together, building and creating our practical world. Fixing broken legs and developing machines that can support those who may need them. But not for fixing minds and beings who are not broken. This responsibility will belong to all of us, recognizing that when one is in dis-ease, we all are. In this vision of a post materialist world, yes there is still suffering – but it takes on different meanings and becomes recognized for its value in taking our hand and reminding us who we are.

When children tell their adult carer they hear voices in their heads or travel outside their bodies, perhaps we would not be so quick to seek medical support. With our post materialist knowledge and growing awareness of reality, time would be taken to explore these experiences with our children. Stigma would dissolve and we could openly turn to our communities of support. Our elders, no longer hidden away in care homes, but brought back into the circle to impart their own wisdom born through experience, as they stand on the threshold of death. This imagining of a post materialist world now needs to be a collective one.

Children's Unexplained Experiences through a Post Materialist Lens

Through the book, I have shown through my own and others' research that many children have a vast array of experiences that challenge usual ideas about reality. The biggest problem children face, now and in the future, is the mainstream physicalist system of thought, that shapes and governs how children and their experiences are understood. Some themes or conclusions reached throughout the book are listed here:

1. Children's natural ways of being are not nurtured or encouraged, in fact the opposite happens through systems such as education. In modern society, children's coercion and immersion into a system, counter to their natural ways of being, alienates children from their own source of happiness.
2. Experiences considered "unexplained" in mainstream thought may be a frequent and a valuable aspect of childhood (whether positive or negative), one that is currently ignored, silenced or diagnosed.
3. Studies show that experiences known as psi are highly likely to be extensions of natural cognitive processes that children use when they cannot verbalize or express what they need to communicate. Although more common in younger children, older children are reporting psi experiences. This may be a compensatory process as

older children are struggling to engage in the world.

4. Children may easily shift into different states of consciousness more conducive to experiencing certain types of phenomena. Everyday activities such as play are often overlooked by adults as potential states of being that demonstrate children's interactions with nonmaterial spaces. Activities for older children, such as video game playing, may account for altered states of consciousness in older children that trigger unexplained experiences.

5. Children may be more easily influenced by a collective consciousness, as their ego boundaries have not yet fully developed. This means, intrusive content into their private fields is not theirs, nor their responsibility. Many children are diagnosed with conditions based on mind activity that is intrusive and repetitive or voices other to their own.

6. We know very little about the mind, matter, self and subjective experiences, yet fixed meanings are assigned to children's unexplained experiences.

7. Current models that are used to explain children's unexplained experiences are inadequate. These are models based on a division between the mental and material, ultimately rooted in an idea of the world as physical.

8. Children are consciously challenging the current status quo through their experiences and ways of being. The status quo is based on western cultural belief systems that are disconnected from their own origins. Some children's experiences correspond with old western cultural narratives and non-western systems of thought.

9. There are no supportive spaces for children's transitional, transformational and unexplained experiences in western culture. As adults are disconnected from their

own indigenous knowledges, so too are children – left without mentorship and support for their experiences.

10. Children have the wisdom, insights and capacities to inform post materialist scholarship and should be included in ongoing studies.

I have discussed in previous chapters how some philosophical ideas, such as Kastrup's *analytical idealism*, offer great potentials for reauthoring children's unexplained experiences and ways of being. Kastrup's philosophy can hold and make sense of other scientific propositions covered in the book – such as Jung's collective consciousness and the Grofs' perinatal matrices. Situating the complexities of mental spaces, collective fields and different qualitative experiences, within a simple explanation of the universe as consciousness – corresponding with the living experiences of children and adults – while bringing attention back to the gaping void that has existed between human beings, social life and the natural world. Let us remember, celebrate, return to and explore more, our children and their unexplained experiences, as we move into a post materialist world.

Author Biography

Donna Thomas is an independent researcher and a Research Fellow at the University of Central Lancashire in the UK. Donna has a PhD in Linguistics and Identity awarded from Lancaster University and teaches postgraduate students in her current role. Donna has researched with children and young people since 2004 in local government, community and academic settings. For the past several years, Donna has been researching the nature of self and unexplained experiences with children, as an independent and academic researcher. Donna has published academic papers and public interest articles and was awarded *best paper* for her presentation "Child as Alter" in 2019 by the Consciousness and Experiential Section of the British Psychological Society.

Donna's research was motivated by an NDE type experience at the age of 15, that led to her experiencing a range of anomalies. This motivated Donna to challenge mainstream systems of thought that label unexplained experiences of children as disorder, without first exploring them with children. Donna works with children and academics across the world, still actively researching children's unexplained experiences and the nature of self.

Donna voluntary supports children and young people who find themselves in crisis or who just want to share their unexplained experiences. She volunteers in school settings and runs a website "A Children's Guide to the Unknown", to develop spaces for children to share their experiences and learn about different ways to understand their experiences.

Note to Reader

Thank you for purchasing *Children's Unexplained Experiences in a Post Materialist World*. My hope is that you have enjoyed and taken something valuable from reading the book, as I have in creating it. If you have a few moments, please feel free to add your review of the book to your favorite online site for feedback. Also, if you would like to connect with other books that I have coming in the near future, please visit my website for news on upcoming works, recent blog posts and to sign up for my newsletter:

https://drdonnamthomas.com/

Endnotes

An Introduction
1. David Chalmers, 1994
2. There is debate about the authenticity of the sisters' experiences.
3. Meet the young people who believe they're communicating with the dead. Why are some millennials turning to the supernatural? Vicky Spratt, BBC, 5 March 2019
4. see Irwin, 1993 – cited in Lawrence et al, 1995
5. see De Leyn et al, 2021
6. see Ian Stevenson, 1977; Jim Tucker, 2008
7. see Article 12, United Nations Convention, Rights of the Child

Chapter 1
8. https://www.kidspot.com.au/parenting/your-child-could-be-psychic/news-story/bda93238f4ad7924560c3864 efea1a3a – Athina Bailey, 2021
9. see Norman Fairclough, 2003
10. UK Parliamentary Report, Children and Young People's Mental Health, June 2021
11. see Racine et al, 2021
12. see Polanczyk et al, 2010
13. see Kelleher & Cannon, 2011
14. see McGrath et al, 2015
15. see Roxburgh & Roe, 2014
16. see Gabor Mate, 2014
17. see Breeding & Baughman, 2003
18. see https://www.olivermcgowan.org/
19. see Phil Borges TED Talk: https://www.youtube.com/watch?v=CFtsHf1lVI4
20. see James Hillman, 1975

21. see Ed Hoffman, 1998
22. see Joseph Campbell, 1968
23. see Melvin Morse, 1983
24. see Alvarado, 2000
25. see Mossbridge & Radin, 2018

Chapter 2

26. https://www.bbc.co.uk/news/world-us-canada-57325653
27. The Union of Ontario Indians based on research compiled by Karen Restoule.
28. see The Print, November 2021
29. see Raven Grimassi, 1999, 11
30. see Raven Grimassi, 1999, 11
31. see Raven Grimassi, 1999, 12
32. see Trousdale, 2013
33. see Trousdale, 2013
34. see Nehemiah & Turnip, 2018
35. see Legare et al, 2012
36. see www.alittlechildshallleadus.com/social-justice
37. see Grob & Dobkin, 1994
38. see Thomason, 2010
39. see Amoss, 1978
40. see Schumaker, 1995
41. see Thomason, 2010
42. see Ally & Yew-Siong, 2020
43. see Stan & Christina Grof, 1990
44. see Stan Grof, 2012
45. see Yust, 2014
46. see Ionas, 2015
47. see Gackenbach, 2006
48. see Gackenbach, 2006
49. see Dauphin & Heller, 2010
50. see Cobb, 2007
51. see Morley, 2018

52. see Cromby et al, 1996

Chapter 3

53. see Society for Psychical Research
54. see Rhine, 1953
55. see Foster, 1943
56. see Drewes, 1991
57. see Anderson, 1960, in White, 1987
58. see Krippner, 1965
59. see Bowers et al, 1990
60. see Hallman

Chapter 4

61. see Krippner, 1974
62. see Jung, 1969
63. http://www.agnesian.com/page/savant-syndrome-faqs
64. see Wendy Chung TED Talk: https://www.ted.com/talks/ wendy_chung_autism_what_we_know_and_what_we_ don_t_know_yet?language=en
65. see Stillman, 2006 – cited by Drewes, 2006
66. see Sheldrake, 1998
67. "An Atheist Doctor's NDE - Graeme O'Connor", NDE Radio: https://www.youtube.com/watch?v=UJzT5qAoMQU
68. see Ring, 1998
69. see Atwater, 2003
70. see Widdison, 2001
71. see *New York Times*, September 1999
72. see Stevenson, 2005
73. see Stevenson, 2005
74. see Tucker, 2000
75. see Tucker, 2000
76. see Keil, 2010
77. see Kuhn, 1962

Chapter 5

78. see Thomas, 2020
79. see Marina Jones, 2014, Futurism
80. see Kress, 1993
81. see Anning et al, 1997
82. see Luke, 2010

Chapter 6

83. see Albahari, 2019
84. see Darling, 1994
85. Jeanette Irons: https://www.massey.ac.nz/~wwpapajl/evolution/assign2/JI/jp.html
86. see Evans, 2013
87. see Oswell, 2016
88. see Wilber, 1984
89. see Washburn, 1995
90. see Rae, 2020
91. see Coddington et al, 2021
92. see Rupert Spira, 2017
93. see Braidotti, 2016, 1
94. see Giddens, 1991

Chapter 7

95. see Schmidt & Berkemeyer, 2018
96. see Cardeña et al, 2000
97. see Moyles, 1991
98. see Marks-Tarlow, 2015
99. see Newson et al, 1970
100. see Marks-Tarlow & Haen, 2019
101. see Rosegrant, 2001
102. see Carhart-Harris et al, 2012; Palhano-Fontes et al, 2015
103. see Carhart-Harris et al, 2012; Palhano-Fontes et al, 2015
104. see Previc, 2011
105. see Haggerty et al, 2013

106. see Previc, 2011
107. see Melchert & Proffitt, 1998
108. see William James, 1902, 379
109. see Caillois, 2001, 23
110. see Jung, 1963

Chapter 8

111. see Dunn & Michaud, 2012
112. see Ahmari and Dougherty, 2015
113. see Lai et al, 2019
114. see Galanter, 1976
115. see Kastrup, 2021
116. see Mercer, 2003
117. see Freud, 1918 – cited in Mercer, 2003
118. see Mercer, 2003
119. see Jung, 1923/1953 – cited in Mercer, 2003
120. see Jung, 1931/1954, 41
121. see Olivetti, 2015, 99
122. see Grof, 1990, 37
123. see Sheldrake, 2009
124. see Sheldrake, 2013, 321
125. see Victor Petrenko, Essentia Foundation

Chapter 9

126. see Duijl et al, 2014
127. see Duijl et al, 2014
128. see Neuner et al, 2012
129. see Igreja et al, 2010
130. see Bourguignon, 1976
131. see Dunn et al, 2016
132. see King et al, 2015
133. see Fehr, 2006
134. see Radin & Rebman, 1996
135. see Thomas, 2021

136. see Yehuda, 2016
137. see Yehuda, 2016
138. https://onbeing.org/programs/rachel-yehuda-how-traum a-and-resilience-cross-generations-nov2017/
139. see Moriera-Almeida et al, 2008; Van Ommeren et al, 2004
140. see Krippner & Achterberg, 2014

Chapter 10

141. see Papineau, 2013
142. see Donald Hoffman interview, Institute for Art and Ideas, 2021
143. see Bernardo Kastrup, 2016
144. see Hameroff & Penrose, 1996
145. see Eccles, 1994
146. see Persinger, 2014
147. see Rouleau, 2014
148. see Huxley, 1999
149. see Barad, 2007
150. see Merewether, 2019
151. see Deleuze, 1987
152. see Claus Metzner, Can a Physicist Embrace Idealism, Essentia Foundation, 15/03/2021
153. see Nash, 1984
154. see Radin, 2018
155. see Barad, 2007
156. see Carr, 2004
157. see Carr, 2004
158. see Carr, 2004

Chapter 11

159. see Matthews, 1994; Murris, 2000
160. see Kitchener, 1990
161. see Murris, 2000
162. see Wittgenstein, 1971 – cited in Murris, 2000

163. see Kant, 1755-1770 (1992)
164. see Piaget, 1929
165. see Kelemen, 2004
166. see Sharon & Woolley, 2004
167. see Woolley et al, 2021
168. see Taylor, 2017; 2021; Hoffman, 1991; Thomas, 2021
169. see William James, 1988
170. see Wittgenstein – cited in Zembylas, 2004, 194
171. see Velmans, 2012, 139
172. see Velmans, 2009, 133
173. see Windt et al, 2016
174. see Arendt, 1971
175. see Albahari, 2019
176. see Chalmers, 1994
177. see Albahari, 2019, 2
178. see Delafield-Butt, 2021
179. see Chalmers, 1994; Goff, 2019
180. see Goff & Moran, 2021
181. see Harris, 2021
182. see Seth, 2013
183. see Wozniak, 2018
184. see Shani & Keppler, 2018
185. see Shani & Keppler, 2018
186. see Kastrup, 2018, 46
187. see Kastrup, 2018, 136
188. see Kastrup, 2018, 136

References

Ahmari, S. and Dougherty, D. (2015). Dissecting OCD Circuits: From animal models to targeted treatments. *Depress Anxiety*, 32: 550-562

Albahari, M. (2019). Perennial Idealism: A Mystical Solution to the Mind-Body Problem. *Philosophers Imprint*, 19(44)

Ally, Y., and Yew-Siong, L. (2020). Religio-cultural Beliefs, and Children Accused of Witchcraft: Describing the child-witch phenomenon. *Child Abuse Research in South Africa*, 21(2)

Alvarado, CS (2000). Out-of-body experiences. In Cardeña, E., Lynn, SJ, & Krippner, S. (eds.), *Varieties of Anomalous Experience: Examining the Scientific Evidence*, pp. 183-218. American Psychological Association

Amoss, P. (1978). *Coast Salish Spirit Dancing*. Seattle: University of Washington Press

Anderson, ML and White, RA (1958). A Survey of Work on ESP and Teacher Pupil Attitudes. *Journal of Parapsychology*, 22, 246-268

Anning, A. (1997). Drawing Out Ideas: Graphicacy and young children. *International Journal of Technology and Design Education*, 7, 219-239

Arendt, H. (1971). *Between Friends. The Correspondence of Hannah Arendt and Mary McCarthy 1949-1975*, ed. C. Brightman (1995). New York: Harcourt Brace

Atwater, PMH (2003). *The New Children and Near-Death Experiences*. Simon & Schuster

Barad, K. (2007). *Meeting the Universe Halfway: Quantum Physics and the Entanglement of Matter and Meaning*. London: Duke University Press

Bierman, DJ (1985). A Retro and Direct PK Test for Babies with the Manipulation of Feedback: A first trial independent replication using software exchange. *Journal of Parapsychology*,

22, 246-390

Bourguignon, E. (1976). *Possession*. San Francisco: Chandler & Sharp

Bowers, K., Regehr, G., Balthazard, C. and Parker, K. (1990). Intuition in the Context of Discovery. *Cognitive Psychology*, 22(1), 72-110

Braidotti, R. (2015). Posthuman Affirmative Politics. In Wilmer, SE and Žukauskaitė, A. (eds.), *Resisting Biopolitics*. London: Routledge

Braud, W. (1981). Psychokinesis Experiments with Infants and Young Children. In WG Roll & J. Beloff (eds.), Research in Parapsychology, 30-3. Metuchen, NJ: Scarecrow Press

Breeding, J. and Baughman, F. (2003). Informed Consent and the Psychiatric Drugging of Children. *Journal of Humanistic Psychology*, 43(2), 50-64

Caillois, R. (1961). *Man, Play and Games*. University of Illinois Press

Campbell, J. (1968). *The Hero with A Thousand Faces*. California: New World Library

Cardeña, E., Lynn, S., & Krippner, S. (2014). *Varieties of Anomalous Experience: Examining the Scientific Evidence*. American Psychological Association, doi.org.10.1037.cns0000093

Carhart-Harris, R., Erritzoe, D., Williams, T., Stone, J., Reed, LJ, Colasanti, A., Tyacke, R., Leech, R., Malizia, A., Murphy, K., Hobden, P., Evans, J., Fielding, A., Wise, R. and Nutt, D. (2012). Neural Correlates of the Psychedelic State as Determined by fMRI Studies with Psilocybin. *PNAS*, 109(6), 2138-2143

Carr, BJ (2004). Mind and the Cosmos. In Lorimer, D. (ed.), *Science, Consciousness and Ultimate Reality*, pp. 33-64. Imprint Academic

Chalmers, DJ (1995). Facing Up to the Problem of Consciousness. *Journal of Consciousness Studies*, 20, 200-219

Chan, YF (2017). Psi Research in China. Psi Encyclopedia.

London: The Society for Psychical Research

Cobb, S. (2007). Virtual Environments Supporting Learning and Communication in Special Needs Education. *Topics in Language Disorders*, 3, 211-225

Coddington, R., Catling, C. and Homer, C. (2020). Seeing birth in a new light: The transformational effect of exposure to homebirth for hospital-based midwives. Midwifery, 88, p.102755

Cohen, E. (2007). *The Mind Possessed: The Cognition of Spirit Possession in an Afro-Brazilian Religious Tradition.* Oxford University Press on Demand

Darling, J. and Van de Pijpekamp, M. (1994). Rousseau on the Education, Domination and Violation of Women. *British Journal of Education Studies*, 42(2), 115-132

Dauphin, B. and Heller, G. (2010). Going to Other Worlds: The Relationships between Videogaming, Psychological Absorption and Daydreaming Styles. *Cyberpsychology, Behavior and Social Networking*, 13(2), 169-172

Delafield-Butt, J. (2021). Autism and panpsychism: Putting process in mind. *Journal of Consciousness Studies*, 28(9-10), 76-90

Deleuze, G. and Guattari, F. (1987). *A Thousand Plateaus: Capitalism and Schizophrenia.* London: Continuum

Doyle, AC (1922). The Coming of the Fairies: The Cottingley Incident. Hodder & Stoughton

Drewes, A. & Drucker, S. (1991). *Parapsychological Research with Children.* New Jersey: Scarecrow Press

Drewes, A. (2002). Dr. Louisa Rhine's Letters Revisited: The Children. *Journal of Parapsychology*, 66(4), 343-370

Dunn, G. and Michaud, N. (2012). *The Hunger Games and Philosophy: A Critique of Pure Treason.* Blackwell

Eason, C. (1999). Mother Link: Stories of Psychic Bonds between Mother and Child. Ulysses Press

Eccles, JC (1994). The Evolution of Complexity of the Brain with the Emergence of Consciousness. In *How the SELF Controls Its BRAIN*, pp. 125-143. Berlin, Heidelberg: Springer

Evans, B. (2013). How autism became autism: The radical transformation of a central concept of child development in Britain. *History of the Human Sciences*, 26(3):3-31

Fairclough, N. (2003). *Analysing Discourse: Textual Analysis for Social Research*. London: Routledge

Fisk, G. (1951). ESP Experiments with an Infant as Subject. *Journal for Psychical Research*, 36, 502

Foster, AA (1943). ESP Tests with American Indian Children. *Journal of Parapsychology*, 7, 94-103

Gackenbach, J. (2006). Video game play and lucid dreams: Implications for the development of consciousness. *Dreaming*, 16(2), 96-110

Galanter, M. (1976). The "Intoxication State of Consciousness": A Model for Alcohol and Drug Abuse. *American Journal of Psychiatry*, 133(6), 635-640

Giddens, A. (1991). *Modernity and Self-identity: Self and Society in the Late Modern Age*. California: Stanford University Press

Goff, P. and Moran, A. (2021). Is Consciousness Everywhere? Essays on Panpsychism. *Journal of Consciousness Studies*, 28(9-10)

Grimassi, R. (1999). The Wiccan Mysteries: Ancient Origins and Teachings. Llewellyn Books

Grob, CS, and Dobkin de Rios, M. (1994). Hallucinogens, Managed States of Consciousness, and Adolescents: Cross-cultural Perspectives. In Bock, PK (ed.), *Handbook of Psychological Anthropology*, pp. 315-329. Praeger Publishers/ Greenwood Publishing Group. (Reprinted in modified form from *Journal of Drug Issues*, 22(1), 1992, 121-138.)

Grof, S. and Grof, C. (2009). *Holotropic Breathwork: A New Approach to Self-Exploration and Therapy*. New York: SUNY Press

Grof, S. (2012). *Healing Our Deepest Wounds: The Holotropic*

Paradigm Shift. Stream of Experience Productions

Haggerty, MK (2013). *An evaluation of a yoga and creative arts program for incarcerated female youth*. [Order No. 1544916]. Saint Mary's College of California

Hallman, CJ (2005). Measuring Children's Intuition in a School Setting. International Journal of Healing and Caring, 5(3)

Hameroff, S. and Penrose, R. (1996). Orchestrated reduction of quantum coherence in brain microtubules: A model for consciousness. *Mathematics and Computers in Simulation*, 40(3-4), 453-480

Hardy, A. (1966). *The Divine Flame*. London: Collins

Harris, A. (2021). A Solution to the Combination Problem and the Future of Panpsychism. *Journal of Consciousness Studies*, 28(9), 129-140

Hillman, J. (1975). *Re-Visioning Psychology*. Harper & Row

Hoffman, D. (2008). Conscious realism and the mind-body problem. *Mind and Matter*, 6(1), 87-121

Hoffman, E. (1998). Peak experiences in childhood: An exploratory study. *Journal of Humanistic Psychology*, 38(1), 109-120

Huxley, A. (1999). *Moksha: Aldous Huxley's Classic Writings on Psychedelics and the Visionary Experience*, eds. M. Horowitz and C. Palmer. Rochester, VT: Park Street Press

Igreja, V., Dias-Lambranca, B., Hershey, D., Racin, L., Richters, R. and Reis, R. (2010). The epidemiology of spirit possession in the aftermath of mass political violence in Mozambique. *Social Science & Medicine*, 71, 3, 592-599

Ionas, G. (2015). Video Games and the Internet and their Effects upon the Brain of Children and Adolescents. *Journal of Business Economics and Information Technology*, 2(6)

James, W. (1988). *William James: Writings 1902-1910: The Varieties of Religious Experience/Pragmatism/A Pluralistic Universe/The Meaning of Truth*. Library of America, William James Edition

Jung, CG (1931). The Stages of Life. *The Structure and Dynamics* of the Psyche, Volume 8. The Collected Works of Carl Jung

Jung, CG (1961). Memories, Dreams, Reflections: An autobiography. Fontana Press

Jung, CG (1969). The Structure and Dynamics of the Psyche. Princeton: Princeton University Press

Kant, I. (1992). Theoretical Philosophy, 1755-1770, trans. and ed. David Walford. Cambridge University Press

Kastrup, B. (2016). The Physicalist Worldview as Neurotic Ego-Defense Mechanism. SAGE Open, 6(4)

Kastrup, B. (2018). The Universe in Consciousness. Journal of Consciousness Studies, 25 (5), 125-155

Kastrup, B. (2019). The Idea of the World: A multi-disciplinary argument for the mental nature of reality. Iff Books

Kastrup, B. (2021). Decoding Jung's Metaphysics: The archetypal semantics of an experiential universe. Iff Books

Keil, J. (2010). Questions of the Reincarnation Type. Journal of Scientific Exploration, 24 (1), 79-99

Kelemen, D. (2004). Are Children "Intuitive Theists"?: Reasoning About Purpose and Design in Nature. Psychological Science, 15(5):295-301

Kelleher, I. and Cannon, M. (2011). Psychotic-like experiences in the general population: Characterizing a high risk group for psychosis. Psychological Medicine, 41(1), 1-6

King, L., Roe, CA and Roxburgh, EC (2015). A transpersonal exploration of epilepsy & its numinous, cosmic states. Paper presented to: Psychology Postgraduate Affairs Group (PsyPa) Annual Conference, University of Glasgow, 22-24 July 2015.

Kitchener, RF (1990). Do Children Think Philosophically? Metaphilosophy, 21(4), 416-431

Kress, G. (1993). Against Arbitrariness: The social production of the sign as a foundational issue in Critical Discourse Analysis. Discourse & Society, 4(2), 169-191

Krippner, S. (1965). Coding and Clairvoyance in a Dual Aspect Test with Children. Perceptual and Motor Skills, 20(3), 745-748

Krippner, S. (1974). *Telepathy*

Kristeva, J. (1980). The Bounded Text. In Roudiez, LS (ed.), *Desire in Language: A Semiotic Approach to Literature and Art*, pp. 36-63. New York: Columbia University Press

Kuhn, T. (1962). Historical Structure of Scientific Discovery: To the historian discovery is seldom a unit event attributable to some particular man, time, and place. *Science*, 136 (3518), 760-76

Kuhn, T. (1966/1996). *The Structure of Scientific Revolutions*. Chicago: University of Chicago Press

Lacan, J. (1981). *Seminar XI: The Four Fundamental Concepts of Psychoanalysis*, ed. JA Miller. New York: Norton

Lai, D., Wetherill, L., Bertelsen, S., Carey, C., Kamarajan, C., and Kapoor, M. et al (2019). Genome-wide association studies of alcohol dependence, DSM-IV Criterion Count and Individual Criteria. *Genes, Brain and Behaviour*, 18(6)

Laroi, F., Van der Linden, M. and Goeb, J-L (2006). Hallucinations and Delusions in Children and Adolescents. *Current Psychiatry Reviews*, 2 (4)

Lawrence, TE, Edwards, C., Barraclough, N., Church, S. and Hetherington, F. (1995). Modelling Childhood Causes of Paranormal Belief and Experience: Childhood trauma and childhood fantasy. *Personality and Individual Differences*, 19 (2), 2019-215

Legare, C., Evans, EM, Rosengren, KS, and Harris, PL (2012). The Coexistence of Natural and Supernatural Explanations across Cultures and Development. *Child Development*, 83(3), 779-793

Luke, D. (2010). Rock Art or Rorschach: Is there more to entoptics than meets the eye? *Time and Mind: The Journal of Archaeology, Consciousness and Culture*, 3(1), 9-28

Macleod, S., Ferrie, C., Zuberi, S. (2005). Symptoms of Narcolepsy in Children Misrepresented as Epilepsy. *Epileptic Discord*, 7(1), 13-17

Marks-Tarlow, T. (2015). From Emergency to Emergence: The Deep Structure of Play in Psychotherapy. *Psychoanalytic Dialogues*, 25:1, 108-123

Maslow, A. (1970). *Religions, Values, and Peak-Experiences*. New York: Viking

Mate, G. (2003). *When the Body Says No: The Cost of Hidden Stress*. London: Vermilion

Matthews, GB (1994). *The Philosophy of Childhood*. Harvard University Press

McGrath, JJ, Saha, S., Al-Hamzawi, A. et al (2015). Psychotic Experiences in the General Population: A Cross-National Analysis Based on 31,261 Respondents From 18 Countries. *JAMA Psychiatry, 72(7)*

Melchert, C., and Proffitt, A. (1998). Playing in the Presence of God: wonder, wisdom and education. *International Journal of Children's Spirituality*, 3:1, 21-34

Mercer, J. (2003). The Idea of the Child in Freud and Jung: Psychological sources for divergent spiritualities of childhood. *International Journal of Children's Spirituality*, 8(2), 115-132

Merewether, J. (2019). New materialisms and children's outdoor environments: Murmurative diffractions. *Children's Geographies*, 17(1), 105-117

Moody, R. (1992). Family reunions: Visionary encounters with the departed in a modern-day psychomanteum. *Journal of Near-Death Studies*, 11, 83-121

Moreira-Almeida, A., Lotufo-Neto, F., Cardeña, E. (2008). Comparison of Brazilian Spiritist Mediumship and Dissociative Identity Disorder. *The Journal of Nervous and Mental Disease*, 196 (5), 420-424

Morley, C. (2015). Lucid Dreaming: A Beginner's Guide to Becoming Conscious in Your Dreams. Hay House, UK

Morse, M. (1993). A Near-Death Experience in a 7-Year-Old Child. *Am J Dis Child*, 137(10), 959-961

Mossbridge, JA & Radin, D. (2018). Precognition as a form of prospection: A review of the evidence. *Psychology of Consciousness: Theory, Research, and Practice*, 5(1), 78-93

Moyles, J. (1991). *Just Playing?* Open University Press

Murris, K. (2016). *The Posthuman Child: Educational transformation through philosophy with picture books* (Contesting Early Childhood series). London/New York: Routledge

Nash, CB (1984). Quantum physics and parapsychology. *Parapsychology Review*, 15(3), 4-6

Nehemiah, N., Turnip, SS (2018). The prevalence and psychosocial risk factors for psychotic-like experiences (PLE) among high school students in Jakarta. *Asia-Pacific Psychiatry*, 10(9):e12337

Neumann, E. (1972). *The Great Mother: An Analysis of the Archetype*. Princeton: Princeton/Bollingen

Neuner, F., Pfeiffer, A., Schauer-Kaiser, E., Odenwald, M., Elbert, T., & Ertl, V. (2012). Haunted by ghosts: Prevalence, predictors and outcomes of spirit possession experiences among former child soldiers and war-affected civilians in Northern Uganda. *Social Science & Medicine*, 75(3), 548-554

Olivetti, K. (2015). Dimensions of the Psyche. *Jung Journal*, 9(4): 98-124

Oswell, D. (2016). Re-aligning children's agency and re-socialising children in Childhood Studies. In Esser, F., Baadar, M., Betz, T. and Hungerland, B. (eds.), *Reconceptualising Agency and Childhood: New perspectives in childhood studies*, pp. 19-34. London: Routledge

Palhano-Fontes, F., Andrade, K., Tofoli, L., Santos, A., Crippa, J., Hallak, J., Ribeiro, S., de Araujo, D. (2015). The Psychedelic State Induced by Ayahuasca Modulates the Activity and Connectivity of the Default Mode Network. https://doi.org/10.1371/journal.pone.0118143

Papineau, D. (2013). *The Rise of Physicalism*, pp. 182-216. Routledge

Persinger, M. (2003). The Sensed Presence Within Experimental Settings: Implications for the Male and Female Concept of Self. *Journal of Psychology Interdisciplinary and Applied*, 137:1, 5-16

Persinger, M. (2014). Replication of God Helmet experiment and many other of our results. – a Blog by Dr. Michael A. Persinger.

Piaget, J. (1929/2002). Les deux directions de la pensée scientifique. *Arch. des sciences physiques et naturelles*, Volume 11, pp. 145-162. New York: Cambridge University Press

Polanczyk, G., Canino, G., Bauermeister, J., Rohde, L., and Frick, P. (2010). Does the Prevalence of CD and ODD Vary across Cultures? *Social Psychiatry and Psychiatric Epidemiology*, 45, 695-704

Powell, D. (2009). The ESP Enigma: The Scientific Case for Psychic Phenomena. Walker & Co

Previc, F. (2011). Dopamine, Altered Consciousness, and Distant Space with Special Reference to Shamanic Ecstasy. In Cardeña, E. and Winkelman, MJ (eds.), *Altering Consciousness: Multidisciplinary Perspectives*, Volume 2. Praeger

Racine, N., McArthur, B., Cooke, J., Eirich, R., Zhu, J., and Madigan, S. (2021). Global Prevalence of Depressive and Anxiety Symptoms in Children and Adolescents during COVID-19: A Meta-analysis. *JAMA Pediatrics*, 175(11), 1142

Radin, DI, and Rebman, JM (1996). Are phantasms fact or fantasy? A preliminary investigation of apparitions evoked in the laboratory. *Journal of the Society for Psychical Research*, 61, 65-87

Radin, D. (2018). *Entangled Minds: Extrasensory Experiences in a Quantum Reality*. Simon & Schuster

Rae, G. (2020). Maternal and Paternal Functions in the Formation of Subjectivity: Kristeva and Lacan. *Philosophy & Social Criticism*, 46(4), 412-430

Randall, J. (1972). Group ESP experiments with schoolboys. *The*

Journal of Parapsychology, 36(2), 133

Rhine, JB, and Pratt, JG (1957). Parapsychology: Frontier Science of the Mind. Springfield, IL: Charles C. Thomas

Rhine, LE (1953). Subjective Forms of Spontaneous Psi Experiences. Journal of Parapsychology, 17, 77-114

Ring, K. (1998). Book Review: Children of the Light: The Near-Death Experiences of Children, by Cherie Sutherland. New York: Bantam, 1995. *Journal of Near-Death Studies*, 17, 127-132

Rosegrant, J. (2001). The psychoanalytic play state. *Journal of Clinical Psychoanalysis, 10 (3-4), pp. 323-343*

Rouleau, N. and Dotta, BT (2014). Electromagnetic fields as structure-function zeitgebers in biological systems: environmental orchestrations of morphogenesis and consciousness. *Frontiers in Integrative Neuroscience*, 8, 84

Rousseau, JJ (1762). Émile

Roxburgh, E. & Roe, C. (2014). Reframing Voices and Visions using a Spiritual Model. An Interpretive Phenomenological Analysis of Anomalous Experiences in Mediumship. *Journal of Mental Health, Religion & Culture*, 17 (6), 641-653

Schmidt, T. and Berkemeyer, H. (2018). The Altered States Database: Psychometric Data of Altered States of Consciousness. *Frontiers in Psychology*, https://doi.org/10.3389/fpsyg.2018.01028

Schumaker, JF (1995). *The Corruption of Reality*. Amherst, NY: Prometheus Books

Seth, AK (2013). Interoceptive inference, emotion, and the embodied self. *Trends in Cognitive Sciences*, 17(11), pp. 565-573

Shani, I. (2015). Cosmopsychism: A holistic approach to the metaphysics of experience. *Philosophical Papers*, 44(3), 389-347

Shani, I. and Keppler, J. (2018). Beyond combination: how cosmic consciousness grounds ordinary experience. *Journal of the American Philosophical Association*, 4(3), pp. 390-410

Sharon, T. and Woolley, JD (2004). Do monsters dream? Young children's understanding of the fantasy/reality distinction. *British Journal of Developmental Psychology*, 22(2), pp. 293-310

Sheldrake, R. (1998). The Sense of Being Stared At: Experiments in schools. *Journal of the Society for Psychical Research*, 62, 311-323

Sheldrake, R. (2011). *The Presence of the Past: Morphic Resonance and the Habits of Nature*. London: Icon Books

Soal, SG & Bowden, HT (1959). The Mind Readers: Some recent experiments in telepathy. Tijdscuff Voorfilosofie, 21(2)

Spira, R. (2017). *The Nature of Consciousness: Essays on the Unity of Mind and Matter*. Oxford: Shambhala

Stevenson, I. (1977). The Explanatory Value of the Idea of Reincarnation. *The Journal of Nervous and Mental Disease*, 164(5), 305-326

Stevenson, I. (1993). Birthmarks and Birth Defects Corresponding on Deceased Persons. *Journal of Scientific Exploration*, 7(4): 403-410

Stillman, W. (2006). Autism and the God Connection: Redefining the Autistic Experience Through Extraordinary Accounts of Spiritual Giftedness. Sourcebooks, Inc.

Swanson, LR (2018). Unifying Theories of Psychedelic Drug Effects. *Frontiers in Pharmacology*, 9, 172

Talih, F. (2011). Narcolepsy presenting as Schizophrenia: A literature review and two case reports. *Innovations in Clinical Psychology*, 8(4), 30-34

Tanous, A. and Donnelly, K. (2000). Is Your Child Psychic? A Guide for Creative Parents and Teachers. iUniverse

Taylor, S. (2017). Two Modes of Sudden Spiritual Awakening? Ego-Dissolution and Explosive Energetic Awakening. *International Journal of Transpersonal Studies*, 37(2)

Thomas, D. (2020). Who am 'I': Reauthoring self, stories and subjectivity in research with children. *Global Studies of Childhood*, 11(3):230-241

Thomas, D. (2021). A participatory research study to explore the healing potential of children's anomalous experiences. *Explore,* https://doi.org/10.1016/j.explore.2021.8.012

Thomason, TC (2010). The Role of Altered States of Consciousness in Native American Healing. *Journal of Rural Community Psychology,* E13 (1)

Tobert, N. (2018). Cultural U-Turns in Mental Well-Being: Acknowledging the Dilemma. *Journal of Humanistic Psychology,* doi:10.1177/0022167818762916

Trousdale, A. (2013). Embodied spirituality. *International Journal of Children's Spirituality,* 18:1, 18-29

Tucker, JB (2000). A Scale to Measure the Strength of Children's Claims of Previous Lives: Methodology and Initial Findings. *Journal of Scientific Exploration,* 14(4), 571-581

Tucker, JB (2008). Children's Reports of Past-Life Memories: A Review. *Explore,* 4(4), 244-248

Tucker, JB (2016). The Case of James Leininger: An American Case of the Reincarnation Type. *Explore,* 12(3), 200-207

Van Duijl, M., Kleijn, W. and de Jong, J. (2014). Unravelling the spirits' message: a study of help-seeking steps and explanatory models among patients suffering from spirit possession in Uganda. *Int J Ment Health Syst,* 8, 24

Velmans, MA (2009). How to Define Consciousness – and how not to define consciousness. *Journal of Consciousness Studies,* 16, 139-156

Velmans, MA (2012). The Evolution of Consciousness. *Contemporary Social Science,* 7(2) 117-138

Von Petzinger, G. (2017). The First Signs: Unlocking the Mysteries of the World's Oldest Symbols. Atria Books

Wallis, D. (1999). Conversations/Dr. Ian Stevenson; You May Be Reading This In Some Future Past Life. *New York Times,* September 26, 1999

Washburn, M. (1995). *The Ego and the Dynamic Ground.* Albany: SUNY Press

White, R. (1987). Tribute to an Experimenter: Margaret L. Anderson. *The Journal of Parapsychology*, 51(2), 111

Widdison, HA (2001). Book Review: Children of the New Millennium: Children's Near-Death Experiences and the Evolution of Mankind, by P.M.H. Atwater. *Journal of Near-Death Studies*

Wilber, K. (1984). The Developmental Spectrum and Psychopathology: Part I, stages and types of pathology. *Journal of Transpersonal Psychology*, 198

Windt, JM, Nielsen, T. and Thompson, E. (2016). Does Consciousness Disappear in Dreamless Sleep? *Trends in Cognitive Sciences*, 20(12), 871-882

Woolley, JD, Nissel, J. and Gilpin, AT (2021). Children's Use of Testimony to Determine Reality Status. *Child Development*

Wozniak, M. (2018). "I" and "Me": The Self in the Context of Consciousness. *Frontiers in Psychology*, https://doi.org/10.3389/fpsyg.2018.01656

Yehuda, R., Daskalakis, NP, Bierer, LM, Bader, H., Klengal, T., Holsboer, F. and Binder, E. (2016). Holocaust Exposure Induced Intergenerational Effects on FKBP5 Methylation. *Biological Psychiatry*, https://www.biologicalpsychiatryjournal.com/article/S0006-3223(15)00652-6/fulltext

Yust, K-M. (2014). Digital power: exploring the effects of social media on children's spirituality. *International Journal of Children's Spirituality*, 19:2, 133-143

Zeedyk, S. (2021). *Sabre Tooth Tigers & Teddy Bears: The connected baby guide to understanding attachment*. Jessica Kingsley Publications

Zembylas, M. and Michaelides, P. (2004). The Sound of Silence in Pedagogy. *Educational Theory*, 54(2) 193-210

ESSENTIA

Essentia Books, a collaboration between John Hunt Publishing and Essentia Foundation, publishes rigorous scholarly work relevant to metaphysical idealism, the notion that reality is essentially mental in nature. For more information on modern idealism, please visit www.essentiafoundation.org.